More praise for Game of Teams...

"*Game of Teams* is both a timely and relevant read on the power of working with a coach to develop Emotional Intelligence. From Self-Awareness all qualities unfold, including those vital for a team to thrive as well as the leaders who lead them by their own example. Like Jim, the aspiring leader in this book, until we have our experience reflected back to us, we can't see what we can't see. In Jim's case, his coach Toni, becomes the gateway through which he can see himself."

S. MICHELE NEVAREZ, CEO at Goleman, EI

"The leap from individual contributor to team leader can be one of the most significant transitions any employee ever makes. Many fail because they are not prepared, supported, or coached for success. *Game of Teams* is an engaging tale that reveals how powerful the concept of collaboration is to team success and how, with the right support and encouragement, an individual contributor can become a better leader than they ever imagined."

TONY BINGHAM, President & CEO at Association for Talent Development (ATD)

"This is a must-read book for leaders who strive to collaborate and lead teams successfully. Winsor Jenkins shows us through quality storytelling how a leader unlocks the collaboration code by adopting proven practices that guide team collaboration and win-win outcomes."

ENRIQUE G. WASHINGTON, Executive Talent Acquisition Leader for
Fortune 500 Companies, and co-author of *Competencies at Work:*
Providing a Common Language for Talent Management

"When Jim, the lead character, says, 'It sounds like I have to reinvent myself,' the reader shares his hesitancy. Lucky for us, Winsor Jenkins provides a comprehensive guide to just that in his newest book, *Game of Teams*. You would likely read many books and still come up short against the myriad of proven methods Jim's coach, Toni, applies to develop his competence. More important, in this narrative story, they form a systematic and holistic approach for leaders to drive collaboration's development. A must read."

JEFF MCMILLIAN, Director of Labor Relations and HR, Vistra Corp

"Jenkins offers his ideas about collaborative leadership in the form of a story about a manager taking over a bigger role. Its messages about coaching and action-learning are clear and convincing. The focus of the story on the front lines of the organization, rather than the c-suite, makes the book relevant to a wide audience."

LESLIE GOLDENBERG, Hudson Institute Certified Coach

"One of the most common mistakes I see companies make is plopping strong individual contributors into a leadership role without any prior experience or training. *Game of Teams* is an excellent leadership fable that helps demystify this common challenge in a fun, engaging way. The protagonist Jim learns some of my favorite leadership principles and gets practical advice from his own coach about leading teams in a collaborative and effective way. This is a vitally important read for today's upside-down world."

PHILLIP WILSON, President—General Counsel, Labor Relations Institute

GAME
of
TEAMS

Discover
How to Become a
Collaborative Leader

WINSOR JENKINS

Published by: DW Publishing
              Meridian, ID 83642
              wins@winsorjenkins.com
              503-201-0772

Printed in the United States of America

Paperback ISBN: 978-0-9795724-2-5
ebook ISBN: 978-0-9795724-3-2
Library of Congress Control Number: 2020923730

First Edition: 2021
Second Printing: 2024
10 9 8 7 6 5 4 3 2

Cover and interior design: Open Heart Designs, www.openheartdesigns.com

To all those looking for new forms of collaboration and teamwork with the goal of generating win–win outcomes in a highly complex and interdependent world.

2025 AXIOM BUSINESS BOOK AWARD WINNER

⎯ SILVER MEDAL ⎯

Game of Teams: Discover How to Become a Collaborative Leader, won the prestigious 2025 Axiom Business Book Award — Silver Medal, in the Category of Business Stories / Fables.

The Axiom Business Book Awards are the largest and most respected critical guidepost for business books in today's new world of publishing. Previous medalists include Nobel laureate Robert Shiller, former U.S. Secretary of State Condoleezza Rice, Pulitzer Prize winner Doris Kearns Goodwin, philanthropist and investor Raymond Dallo, as well as many other business and thought leaders.

The Axiom Business Book Awards are intended to bring increased recognition to exemplary business books and their creators. Axiom Award winning books are listed by their Gold, Silver, and Bronze medal designations across thirty categories ranging from General Business/Economics to Leadership to Business Ethics, for example. To learn more, go to: www.axiomawards.com

Contents

Author's Note

The great writer Victor Hugo once said, "there is one thing stronger than all the armies in the world, and that is an idea whose time has come." *Game of Teams* introduces the idea that management innovation is needed more than ever to help people on teams learn how to effectively collaborate and function interdependently. With teams and team-based applications continuing to dominate workplace settings, collaboration is essential to help people tackle accelerating and unprecedented levels of change.

Game of Teams promotes an innovative, yet practical team operating platform to develop team leaders. This platform was introduced in my first book, *The Collaborator*, where our global business world is compared to the game of soccer—an environment where people must effectively collaborate to succeed. Embedded in this platform are several team principles to develop a collaborative mind-set and essential competencies to develop a collaborative skill set. The principles come from the game of soccer and mirror a successful soccer team's behavior on the field.

As the story unfolds, we follow the learning and development journey of a newly promoted team manager, Jim Hernandez. He is confronted with the need to develop a nonperforming team. And he must develop a collaborative mind-set and skill set—in real time—to effectively lead his team to collaborate and succeed. With the help of an external coach, Toni Burns, he embarks on a journey that challenges his commitment and confidence to become a collaborative leader. As a trained coach, she helps him progress along his developmental pathway, providing team principles, essential competencies, best practices, along with established and trusted models. Combined, these provide a framework for her to coach Jim, build his commitment and competence, and develop a collaborative mind-set and skill set to crack the collaboration code and succeed.

Acknowledgments

Thanks to my virtual publication team for their collaboration and expertise in making my journey a reality: Linda Gray, for her excellent copyediting; Jamie Tipton (Open Heart Designs), for her innovative design work on the book's cover and layout; Michelle Williams on her diligent proofreading; and Joanne McCall (McCall Media Group) for her strategic guidance and support.

Special thanks also to thought leader Bruce Griffiths (Organization Systems International) for his support, loyalty, and friendship.

Thanks to thought leaders including Gary Hamel, Ken Blanchard, Warren Bennis, Edgar Schein, Daniel Goleman, Pam McLean, William Bridges, Britt Andreatta, and many others who have touched my life and influenced my thinking.

Thanks to all the teams I have been a part of who influenced my thinking since the beginning.

Thanks, too, to my coaching colleagues who continue to strive to make coaching a value-added option for developing leaders and teams. These colleagues include organizations such as the International Coaching Federation and the Hudson Institute of Coaching.

I'd also like to express my appreciation of, and respect for, all of the people who move into new leader roles and embrace development (personal and professional), including coaching, as a way to support their transition and success.

Finally, a big thanks to my wife, Dee Dee, for her continued support.

About the Author

Winsor Jenkins (www.winsorjenkins.com) is a former senior-level leader with three publicly traded companies. He played a key in-house role in the development of leaders at all levels for more than thirty years.

His passion for collaboration began when, too frequently, he found himself trying to persuade people to set aside their focus on win-lose strategies and instead work to generate win-win outcomes. As a result of this experience, he wrote *The Collaborator* in 2007, introducing people to an innovative, yet practical way to collaborate on teams and achieve win-win results.

After leaving the corporate world in 2014, he started his consulting business with a focus on collaborative leadership development and coaching. This led to co-developing *The Collaboration Game* (2016), a team development training program to help people develop a collaborative mind-set and skill set to effectively collaborate.

In 2018 he served as a contributing author, writing Chapter Three — Collaboration, for the Association for Talent Development's (ATD) book, *Focus on Them*.

In 2021 Winsor wrote *Game of Teams* which is a sequel to his first book. In this book, he promotes the importance of coaching to support collaborative leadership and team development.

He has also written articles for the National Soccer Coaches Association of America's publication, Soccer Journal, and the Journal of the Human Resources Planning Society, along with blog posts for ATD, Innovation Excellence, and LinkedIn.

Winsor received his coaching training from the Hudson Institute of Coaching. Along with being certified in the past by the International Coaching Federation (ICF), he held certifications in several leadership and team development training programs, including Situational Leadership. He is certified in a variety of assessment tools used in coaching and leadership development, including Myers-Briggs Type Indicator, EQi-2.0, and Polaris 360.

Winsor is a graduate of Cornell University (BS, Industrial & Labor Relations) and the University of Idaho (MBA).

Introduction

Game of Teams is a story about collaboration and the importance of coaching to become a collaborative leader.

In a world demanding management innovation to solve complex challenges, the significance of collaboration cannot be underestimated. Defined as a marked departure from customary ways in which management's work is performed, it's described herein as a new leader and team development framework. When applied, it helps people harness the power of connections across their team's network to effectively collaborate and produce winning results.

Written in the form of a business allegory, *Game of Teams* leverages the team platform introduced in my book, *The Collaborator*. Here, the global business world is compared to the game of soccer, an environment where people must effectively collaborate to succeed. In soccer, for example, players must be highly competent in adapting to changing conditions, assimilate new information on the run, and apply multiple skills across a network to win — all in real time. In our VUCA[1] world, the same holds true for people working on teams. They too must effectively collaborate to achieve results.

Game of Teams promotes the development of a collaborative mind-set and skill set to help people function interdependently, creating added value for producing win-win outcomes. This is critical

---

1   VUCA is an acronym that is used to describe four general conditions and situations: volatile, uncertain, changing, and ambiguous. Its relevance to leaders in business, for example, is clear, as these conditions are highly descriptive of the environment in which business is conducted every day.

in today's VUCA world where collaborative leadership has vital significance. Indeed, we should all recognize that a collaborative mind-set is no longer a nice to have, but a need to have quality when it comes to team leadership and collaboration. After all, people working on teams are constantly dealing with accelerating—and unprecedented—levels of change!

Embedded in this framework are several novel team principles used to describe a collaborative mind-set. These come the game of soccer and mirror a successful soccer team's behaviors and actions on the field. A series of essential competencies are aligned with the principles; applied, they describe a collaborative skill set. *Game of Teams* introduces the Polaris® Competency Model to support competency development.

Combined, a collaborative mind-set and skill set offers a methodology for generating team trust and psychological safety. Without this, collaboration is impossible.

But teams—and team leaders—can't be expected to effectively develop collaboration skills on their own. Indeed, it requires coaching. Research tells us that a commitment to coaching increases employee engagement, improves productivity, and accelerates the achievement of results. And, without coaching, team performance suffers!

———

As the story unfolds, we follow the learning and development journey of a newly promoted team manager, Jim Hernandez. He is confronted with the need to develop a nonperforming team. And he must develop a collaborative mind-set and skill set—all in real time—to effectively lead his team to collaborate and succeed. With the help of an external coach, Toni Burns, he embarks on a journey that challenges his commitment and confidence to become a collaborative leader. As a trained coach, she helps him progress along his developmental pathway, providing team principles, essential competencies, best practices, along with established and trusted models. Combined, these provide a framework for her to coach Jim, build his commitment and competence, and develop a collaborative mind-set and skill set to crack the collaboration code and succeed. On his journey, he will need coaching to help him:

- develop his self-awareness and emotional intelligence
- tackle blind spots that show up in the form of interpersonal competencies, such as ability to delegate
- be open to feedback on his performance from others, including his coach
- challenge underlying assumptions and values regarding people and teams, if needed
- develop new skills beyond his technical and functional skills, such as leadership flexibility
- understand why relationship building is important, both to his success and to building self-awareness
- learn a new operating platform for leading and managing his team
- lead with a collaborative mind-set made up of a several team principles
- apply a collaborative skill set made up of a series of essential competencies
- create a collaboration culture for his team
- transition to a coaching role as needed to support the team's needs

His journey is a never-ending challenge requiring his personal commitment to learning and development. Although it may not take him places where no one has gone before, it will be a journey on a road less traveled. His commitment to coaching is the key to his success.

PART 1

Collaborative Leader
Development Transition

HUMP DAY

Wednesday. Often described as 'hump day,' it didn't feel like the remainder of this particular week would be all downhill for Jim Hernandez. Since being promoted two weeks ago, from lead tech in product development to manager of information technology field services, he'd started to second-guess why he accepted the position.

"What's it going to take to get people on your team to perform and support sales teams in the field?" Jim's handball partner, Jake, asked as the two men walked out of the gym that evening.

"Good question, Jake. I'm not sure how to answer it. The team has only been functioning for three months. And with the recent resignation of their team leader, there's not a lot of history, if you know what I mean. It will just take time to figure things out. I should learn more once my boss returns from his overseas business trip and we can meet."

"Let me know if I can help once you learn more about your situation," Jake said, walking to his car.

Jim nodded. "Will do."

Jim's new role required him to support four cross-functional teams located in London, Singapore, São Paulo, and Los Angeles. Each team was made up of several salespeople and an information technology, or IT, specialist. The IT specialists reported directly to him. He also had four IT specialists located at his office in Portland, Oregon, who reported to him. Along with product development staff, they were responsible to help develop and implement highly customized computer-based training solutions for customers—which was why a dedicated IT specialist was assigned to each remote office.

Before accepting his new position, Jim had been told by his new supervisor, Brett Logan, that he would need to be comfortable working with cross-functional teams operating virtually under a matrix structure. Brett had also pointed out the need to develop teams that effectively collaborated, since collaboration was critical to product innovation and the company's success. Understanding the dynamics of team formulation, developing productive relationships built on trust, identifying team roles, establishing team goals, and coaching team members as needed would also be required. Most important, he recalled Brett saying, was understanding the importance of *psychological* safety to both the team's well-being and its ability to effectively collaborate. Although Jim had listened intently to what was being described, he realized he really had no idea of what all that meant. "Maybe I should have asked for some clarification," Jim wearily chuckled to himself.

Jim knew that he was still functioning too much as a lead tech to support his team's needs. Yet, he was not clear on how to transition into his new role. In addition, it was becoming clear that Jim's new team was performing poorly—and had been, apparently, since it was formed three months earlier. *I've got to find out what the problem is*, Jim thought.

The challenge to manage his team was already beginning to negatively affect Jim's family life. His wife and two young children had been requiring more of his time at home prior to his promotion. Before, he'd worked a fixed schedule and seldom had weekend duties. Now he was working longer hours each day and coming in over the weekend.

Jim was still thinking about Jake's question when he arrived home and was greeted by his wife, Diane.

"How was your day?" she asked with a concerned look.

KICK-OFF

In the absence of his new supervisor, Jim started to gather feedback from salespeople to understand his team's poor performance. He was told that his people were not focused on supporting sales—or, ultimately, their customers. One salesperson seemed to sum up the general consensus: "It's like they're a band of musicians who are focused on playing their own tune!" Jim also heard that his team members functioned as 'silos' and that they were not reliable. This often left the sales force in embarrassing positions with their customers. So far, Jim realized, he'd found no evidence of any effort on the part of his team to effectively collaborate. And he had no idea how to get them to shape up.

In his search to find possible solutions to his challenge, Jim contacted an old friend. Dan was well respected as a soccer coach at the local high school. He'd taken the girl's soccer team all the way to state finals the previous year. "If anybody knows about getting a team to perform, it's gotta be Dan," he said to himself.

Over the phone, Jim brought his buddy up-to-date on what he was facing at work. "Well, I might have a few ideas that could help," replied Dan. "Tell you what—why don't you come over to watch a soccer game with me on TV tonight, and we can talk about it? And you're in luck—Real Madrid, a truly outstanding team, is playing. They really know how to leverage team values and culture to gain a competitive advantage—and just wait until you see how they collaborate on the field!"

"Dan, I don't know a thing about soccer! But if you say it might help to watch them play, I'll be there."

———

"Great to see you, Jim," said Dan as the two men settled in to watch the soccer match.

"Thanks again for the invite."

Dan nodded. "Glad to help. This should be a good game, and I hope it will give you some ideas."

Although Jim knew little about soccer, he was looking forward to watching Real Madrid play. He'd recently read an article—in a business magazine, no less—about their history and how they had risen to become not only a top sports team, but also one of the world's most successful business organizations. In 2019 *Forbes* listed Real Madrid as the third–most valuable sports team in the world (right behind the Dallas Cowboys and the New York Yankees), with a valuation of $4.2 billion. More impressive, the Spanish soccer team had managed to achieve that level of success in less than twenty years.

"Let me know if you have any question once we get into watching the game," Dan said.

Jim was fascinated with Real Madrid's history. It seemed that the team's *culture* had the greatest impact on performance both on and off the field. Culture meant using collaboration to achieve goals. Today, Jim hoped to learn about collaboration and how it could be developed to generate innovative solutions and support global sales.

———

"How was the game?" Diane asked, as Jim walked in the door.

"I enjoyed it. And it was good to see Dan again."

"Since I don't know anything about soccer, I'm not sure what to ask," she revealed.

Jim paused. "I'm in the same boat. But I think I learned a few things tonight."

"What was the highlight for you?" Diane asked, probing to learn more.

"Well, for one thing, the word 'teamwork' means collaboration these days. When we were growing up, teamwork had a different meaning—perhaps 'cooperating' or 'coordinating' with each other. I'm not sure how to describe the difference. Once I learn more I'll let you know. But to answer your question, for the first time I saw what team collaboration looks like on a playing field."

"That's positive. What's next?"

———

Jim's evening of watching a soccer match got him thinking about what he needed to do to be successful. It was obvious to him that both team coaches had faith in their players to effectively collaborate. As a result, each team functioned in a self-directed way and was able to create and employ innovative strategies to adapt to and manage changing conditions—in real time. This was the behavior Jim wanted to see in his team.

3

HELP IS ON THE WAY

Jim briskly walked down the hall to meet his supervisor, Brett Logan, the company's vice president of information technology. This would be their first scheduled meeting since Jim had been promoted three weeks earlier, and he was hoping to learn more about his team's performance history and Brett's plan for Jim's training and development.

Brett was eager to hear how things were going in Jim's new role. "Who's your favorite leader?" he asked Jim as he settled into his chair.

"Interesting question. I really haven't given it much thought."

"I always viewed Nelson Mandela as my favorite leader. He was someone who was able to inspire, change, and unite people in support of his cause. And that was after spending twenty-seven years in prison!"

"Yeah. I remember watching the movie *Invictus*," Jim said with a smile.

"Good movie. Mandela's success in bringing a nation together using sport was a remarkable accomplishment, to say the least. I would encourage you to read the book to learn more about his journey."

Interesting conversation so far, Jim thought. His relationship with Brett was so new that he knew very little about his background and way of thinking. The idea of talking about leadership was something he hadn't expected today. Perhaps it was Brett's way to break the ice and start the relationship in a productive manner.

"Jim, let's catch up on how things have been going for you since you took on your new role. I was hoping to meet with you earlier, but I had priorities in the field to tackle. You probably felt like I had abdicated my responsibilities. I apologize for that delay."

Jim paused before speaking. "I've been looking forward to meeting with you. So far, it's been a case of 'hurry up and wait,' which is challenging in its own way, if you know what I mean."

"I'm not surprised to hear that. Here's hoping you've hung in there and haven't become disillusioned! Moving from an individual contributor role to a leadership role is a big step that requires your commitment and competence. In fact, your commitment is something that can't be compromised. It needs to be maintained to help develop the competence, or skills, to lead people. On both fronts, it's my job to help you succeed."

"So far, I'm still committed. I've checked out a few things to help me understand how teams function. A friend recommended watching a soccer game to help me understand team collaboration. It was a good experience to see how players on the team collaborated to get results."

"That was a very insightful recommendation. Soccer is a fitting example of an environment where people must effectively collaborate to be successful."

Jim nodded.

Brett was pleased to learn that Jim had taken the initiative to understand how effective teams function. The idea that he had picked up on sport as a way to understand collaboration was another good sign. *Perhaps Mandela's story and its influence on Jim would pay dividends*, he thought. Good on Jim's friend for making the recommendation.

"My game plan moving forward includes bringing in a coach to help you with your transition," Brett explained. "We'll get that process started next week. I will have Human Resources send you a list of coaching candidates to contact and screen. Once you select your coach, we can get started with your development."

Jim was relieved for the moment. "Sounds good, Brett."

———

Two weeks. Not too bad, Jim thought. Finding a coach to help him with his transition was easier than he'd anticipated. With luck, his new coach would be able to get up to speed quickly on the challenges he faced. After all, she had been highly recommended as someone with coaching credentials—and a strong history of coaching teams. She also brought solid senior-level leadership experience from working in a highly respected global organization.

Jim was feeling better about things when he got a call from the front desk that his new coach, Toni Burns, was waiting in the lobby to meet with him.

"Hi, Toni," Jim said, extending his hand to greet her. "Good to see you again."

"Good morning, Jim. Thanks for the selecting me as your coach. I'm looking forward to working with you."

———

Brett was delighted to learn that Jim had moved quickly to select a coach. He knew from personal experience that coaching would help Jim succeed. As Jim's supervisor, he believed it was his responsibility to provide Jim with the appropriate direction and support. By having a coach, Jim would have resources to tackle his development in a productive way.

The past few months had been eventful for Brett. The company had been acquired by another firm, and he'd been nervous about what that might mean for himself, his colleagues, and their customers. Brett was grateful to learn that his new company's leadership was committed to developing a collaborative culture. This included team coaching. *The importance of culture cannot be overstated*, he thought as he prepared to meet with Jim and Toni for the first time.

"Come on in," Brett said, walking to the door to greet Jim and his new coach.

"Good morning," Toni said, sitting down.

Brett paused before speaking. "Good to meet you, Toni. And welcome to the organization."

"Thank you. I'm looking forward to working with Jim and the organization."

"Toni, I thought it would make sense to have this meeting to kick things off in a positive way. You may not be aware that coaching is new to our organization. I can also say that our focus on team development is fairly new, and it's being pursued by the company as one way to support its efforts to build a collaborative culture."

"Sounds like a winning combination!" Toni said emphatically.

"Absolutely. I've had the benefit of having a coach in the past, so I can relate."

"Brett, may I ask what's motivating the company to develop a collaborative culture?"

"Sure. We believe, for us to grow as a company, we have to innovate. It's directly tied to that goal. For example, we need collaboration to generate innovative learning and development solutions for our customers."

"Makes sense," Toni replied. "Innovation comes from many connection points in a team's network that cause existing ideas to be combined in new ways. It doesn't come from individuals."

Jim nodded.

"So, you're obviously looking at product innovation?" Toni said, glancing over at Jim.

"Yes," Brett said, nodding.

"What about *management* innovation?" she asked.

"That too. That's why you were selected as one of the coaching candidates for Jim to interview."

Toni understood that companies often promote their best technical people to leadership positions. She knew that Jim had strong technical skills and he'd been highly successful as an individual contributor working in product development. She also knew he was sought out for this position based on his ability to work with others to achieve results. Although Jim had limited experience working on a team, he would be charged with developing one that effectively collaborated to produce results. This included coaching people on his team.

Toni understood that taking on a leadership role for the first time is challenging and most people struggle to master their new responsibilities as a leader. The reasons for this vary, but they are usually related to a lack of self-awareness, inadequate training, and lack of coaching. Toni suspected things with Jim would not be any different and he would need help in all these areas.

In order for Jim to succeed, he would need to embrace the idea of developing a collaborative mind-set, which would allow him to become a collaborative leader. Unfortunately, there were no 'secrets' to offer him on his developmental journey. Achieving success would take hard work—and his commitment, competence, and courage would all be tested along the way.

4

DENALI

"Jim, what excites you most about the future of your team?" Toni asked, jumping in to start their first coaching session.

Jim pondered Toni's question. "I've been thinking about that a lot over the past few weeks. For me, it's all about the possibilities that collaboration can produce for the organization."

Toni was curious. "Please, tell me more."

"I guess for my team, the endgame is to really function like a soccer team, finding ways to collaborate to innovate and produce results."

"Soccer is good example of a game—and environment—where people must 'collaborate to innovate' to produce results. Collaboration here really means that players function interdependently on the field, harnessing the power of connections across the team's network to score goals and win."

"That's what I recall seeing when I was at Dan's house watching the Real Madrid game!"

"I'm not surprised to hear that," Toni said, reaching over to her bag. "In order for you and your team to effectively collaborate—say, as Real Madrid does—you'll need to apply all of the team principles that mirror a successful soccer team's actions and behaviors on the field."

"Sounds interesting. Do you have a list of these principles to share?"

"Absolutely," Toni said, handing her list to Jim.

TEAM PRINCIPLES

- Focus On Team
- Understand That Everyone Can Play
- Embrace Diversity
- Rely On Each Other
- Promote Individual & Team Values
- Seek Out Skillful, Adaptable Players
- Charge The Team To Perform The Work
- Empower Players To Win
- Coach Teams To Respond To Changing Conditions On Their Own
- Develop Partners On The Field
- Achieve Cross-Cultural Agility

Jim nodded, scanning the list.

"My job as your coach is to demonstrate how these novel, team principles 'play out' and support your team's ability to collaborate," reassured Toni.

"Sounds compelling. I can't wait to get started."

"Great. We'll be working on that soon."

Toni firmly believed that these team principles, employed by coaches of successful soccer teams, offered an innovative and practical platform for managing teams in today's VUCA world. After all, there was no denying that today's teams must be highly competent in adapting to changing conditions, assimilating new information on the run, and applying multiple skills across a network to achieve results.

Jim smiled. "Brett also mentioned soccer when I met with him."

"Glad to hear that. For me, soccer also works well as an effective *aspirational* metaphor for the organization. I use this metaphor quite a bit in my team coaching."

"Makes sense. I recently read a *Forbes* article that described soccer as the sport of choice for millennials in North America."

"I didn't see that article. But I'm not surprised, since millennials typically bring a global perspective coupled with a more inclusive nature and a sense of comfort with flatter organizational structures like the matrix structure you're working under."

"Don't they also view teamwork as important? I think they're more accustomed to collaborating online, especially when it involves learning."

"That too," Toni said, knowing that Jim, a millennial himself, was most likely referring to his own experience.

———

"What's the boulder—or tough part—of making this shift to achieve your desired outcome?" Toni asked as the two picked up the conversation after a quick coffee break.

"That's another interesting question, Toni," Jim said, glancing toward the window.

"Perhaps there's another metaphor I can share to help?"

"Go for it," Jim said, pushing back in his chair.

Toni nodded. "A metaphor I often use with clients is mountain climbing. For example, climbing Denali is a challenge, to say the least. It starts with establishing a base camp, then moving to a series of higher-level camps that eventually get you to the summit. This involves planning and preparing well in advance for the challenge. Because mountain climbing is a process that gradually grows and gathers momentum, it can be used by you and your group to understand the challenge of building a collaborative team."

Jim smiled. "I like it. I've used this metaphor in the past."

"Perfect. Moving forward, we'll continue to use it, spending time establishing your base camp before moving to higher-level camps. That way, we can effectively deal with any 'boulders,' or obstacles, that get in the way of your future development—and they will!"

Jim knew that Toni's use of metaphors was beneficial. He suspected that good coaches use metaphors frequently as maps to help people reach their destinations. He was happily surprised to hear Toni talk about using soccer as a metaphor to understand collaborative teamwork.

"Jim, one more point to cover this morning before wrapping things up."

Jim nodded.

"As you may know, more work is done by teams these days—often virtually—and that trend is only going to continue. Collaboration's application across our highly complex business world to produce win-win outcomes is what I like to call the, 'game of teams!'"

Jim listened intently to Toni's words.

"I often contrast this to the leadership style practiced throughout the Industrial Revolution, for example," Toni stated.

"What style was that?"

"Playing a win-lose game versus a win-win game was demonstrated time after time using a top-down, command and control style to produce results. Its roots can be found in both the church and the military.

"And you're suggesting that it's no longer appropriate."

"Spot-on Jim. The leadership required in a VUCA world is far beyond the scope of a single leader!"

Toni believed today's VUCA world requires management innovation to tackle the task of developing teams that effectively collaborate. Described as a marked departure from customary ways in which management's work is performed, management innovation was, Toni knew, the key to success in the twenty-first century. The principles, processes, protocols, and practices used in the past that promoted a top-down, command-and-control style were not going to work anymore. This thinking had been echoed for some time now by numerous management professionals and scholars. They'd made it clear that the leadership required in a world that demands interdependence to solve complex challenges is far beyond the scope of a single individual operating with a top-down, chain-of-command style. Obviously, Brett and other senior leaders in the company understood this, along with the need to develop leaders who operated with a collaborative mind-set to succeed going forward.

————————

"How did things go today with your new coach?" Diane asked, walking up to greet Jim as he entered the house that evening.

"Pretty well. Toni asked some good questions and was able to get me thinking about future developmental challenges. She seems to be very insightful."

"How so?"

"Toni used a few metaphors to help me look at the big picture. I believe it was useful to get her perspective. And she used metaphors to help establish our relationship, which was good."

Diane wanted to learn more. "What stood out for you?"

She mentioned the game of soccer as a metaphor, which caught me by surprise. Having seen the Real Madrid game with Dan, I can appreciate its value.

"So, seeing is believing, I guess."

Smiling, Jim nodded.

"Anything else?"

"She talked about mountain climbing as another metaphor for understanding my development process, along with my team's."

Pondering the image, Diane asked, "What's the summit look like?"

"Toni wants me to play a 'game of teams,'" Jim said, grinning slyly, flattered that Diane always seemed interested to hear about his work.

"What's that mean?"

"Basically, that getting to the summit is a win-win proposition, and that you have to collaborate as a team if you want to reach it!"

PART 2

Collaborative Leader Coaching Challenges

5

CHANGING MIND-SETS

The idea of having a coach to help with his transition was something Jim valued. He was hoping Toni would not only help with his leadership and team development efforts, but also be able to help develop his coaching skills.

Earlier, Toni had mentioned that a collaborative mind-set was no longer a 'nice to have,' but a '*need* to have' quality to effectively function as a leader in today's VUCA world. Because of the accelerating and unprecedented levels of change taking place, collaborative leadership has vital significance when it comes to solving complex challenges. Yesterday's 'Lone Ranger,' top-down, command-and-control leadership style worked well for many during the Industrial Revolution, but it simply was not an effective way to master the challenges—or seize the opportunities—that the twenty-first century presented.

"Toni, what makes collaboration so challenging to learn?" Jim asked, returning from lunch.

"Great question, Jim. It's one that I often hear in my coaching work. The short answer may be centered on the underlying assumptions and values people hold that promote individual responsibility and performance over team values and performance. Collaboration also presents an organizational challenge. In fact, I often tell my clients that, just as good may be the enemy of great, individual values can be the enemy of organizational values such as teamwork."

"I think I can relate. I competed in various activities, including sports, in high school, and I experienced conflict. We all like to say there is no 'I' in team, yet we had to deal with it all the time!"

Toni paused before responding. "Well Jim, there is actually an 'I' in team. It shows up in the form of the individual values people bring to the group. People are often surprised to hear me say that, but understanding this truth is key to developing team collaboration."

"OK, say more, Toni."

"The development challenge here is to learn how to deal with team and individual values not in an either-or way, but by understanding that *both* **individual and team values** are needed in order to perform."

"You just mentioned one of our team principles."

"Glad you noticed, Jim!"

Jim smiled.

Toni continued. "Let's use the idea of soccer as a way to understand how we reconcile this values conflict. In soccer, each player brings to the team individual values. When those values are harnessed in a way that supports the team's purpose and works to help the team achieve its goals, those individual values can help players make their own distinctive contributions to the team. And part of harnessing those individual values involves developing players' skills."

"I'm hearing you say that individual and team values—and skills—interact on the field. Correct?"

"Yes. Each player's sense of individual accountability to the team, for example, promotes learning in the form of individual skills that ultimately determine the team's overall skill set and level of performance. Once in play, the coach has the ability to cycle back to identify both individual and team development gaps to ensure that the process for producing team results is working."

"Makes sense now."

"Bottom line—we're talking about **relying on each other** and **emphasizing team success instead of individual success**."

"You just mentioned two more principles!"

"Spot-on, Jim." Toni continued to push on. "Most of us don't really have a solid understanding of what collaboration actually means. We think it means cooperating or coordinating, which I describe as 'group work.' That is not collaboration. This disconnect is one part of the long answer to your question, and it helps explain why developing 'genuine' team collaboration has been an ongoing challenge in organizations."

"So, you're suggesting that collaboration is not in our DNA."

Toni paused before replying. "Short of a situation where people are dealing with a crisis, for example, and their survival is at risk, you seldom see collaboration come into play or applied spontaneously. People tend to collaborate only once they recognize that interdependence is needed to effectively deal with the complexity associated with their challenge."

"Wow! This really makes it sound as though we need to shift our way of thinking."

"Because we are dealing with changing mind-sets here, the challenge to develop team collaboration is huge. In fact, for that reason, my coaching focuses on developing a collaborative mind-set before developing a collaborative skill set."

"Developing mind-set *before* skill set, you say," mused Jim.

"Again, yes. Because our mind-set helps shape the choices we make when it comes to managing our competence, or skill set, it's important to align our mind-set and our skill set such that we are leveraging both to produce win-win outcomes."

Pondering, Jim thought Toni's insights seemed right on target.

"'Lead with mind-set' would be a good way to describe how this alignment process plays out on the job," Toni clarified.

He nodded. "I think I've got it."

"Great. But there's more to this equation to learn. We will get to that soon."

Jim recalled, as a young boy playing sports, he'd often heard the phrase 'may the best team win.' Looking back, he realized that he and his friends had come to expect it as if it were just part of a coin-flip ritual. He could not have imagined how the phrase would have real meaning in today's VUCA world. The fact that team collaboration was needed to effectively compete meant he could not fall back on old habits such as promoting individual values at the expense of team values under the mistaken assumption that teamwork meant merely cooperation or coordination.

————

"How's it going, Jim?" Dan asked, sitting down to grab a bite to eat that evening.

"So far, so good, Dan."

Dan was curious. "How's your new coach working out?"

"Great. In fact, I could not make it without her help. She even introduced me to the idea of using soccer's metaphor!"

Dan grinned. "Wow! Sounds like she's got your team's development all figured out."

"Perhaps."

6

CONNECT SOME DOTS

"What limiting assumptions might you be making that preclude other possibilities when it comes to team collaboration?" Toni asked Jim when they met two days later to continue their conversation.

Jim paused and swallowed before responding. "Not sure if I understand your question."

"Do you believe, for example, in the potential of people to get the job done?"

"Absolutely. But I have to admit I've never given it much thought, Toni."

"Most people don't. But it's important to check your underlying assumptions to make sure they are aligned with what it takes to support and develop people on teams."

"So, believing in the potential of people is obviously important. What does that look like?"

"It's described as having positive underlying assumptions versus negative underlying assumptions. Positive assumptions bolster our willingness to delegate to others, which is a key competency when it comes to managing people."

"It's hard to hand things over to people if you don't trust them," Jim replied, hoping to confirm what he'd heard Toni state.

"Yes. This is the first step to achieve your desired outcome. I often share the story about New United Motor Manufacturing, Inc., or NUMMI, to help reinforce the significance of underlying assumptions about worker behavior and performance. I think it's one of the best stories to describe the consequences of positive underlying assumptions versus negative assumptions in a workplace." Reaching over, Toni handed Jim a piece of paper describing the story.

NUMMI

In the mid-1980s Toyota and General Motors established the joint venture NUMMI (New United Motor Manufacturing, Inc.) in Fremont, California. The goal was to reopen a former GM plant—which had employed what was called "the worst workforce in the U.S. automobile industry" because of its frequent strikes, intentional sabotage, and high absentee-ism rates—and create high-quality products at low cost by implementing a management philosophy called the Toyota Way. Contrary to GM's application of Theory X, an author-itarian philosophy of managing via negative assumptions (e.g., "people dislike work"), the Toyota Way represented a system in which respect and teamwork were the key tenets that guided leadership in identifying problems and making improvements. By changing the plant's culture to one built on mutual trust, Toyota was able to turn a highly dysfunctional car manufacturing plant into a success. And they did it with the same GM people!

Jim looked up at his coach. "Great story, Toni! I can see why you share it with your clients."

"Thanks, Jim. It really drives home the power of underlying assumptions." Jim nodded in agreement.

Toni continued. "I have a business partner who likes to use the image of an iceberg to illustrate this point. As you know, most of an iceberg's mass is below the surface of the water; what we see above the surface is just a small portion of it. He says that qualities such as personality, values, and underlying assumptions are all part of the 'unseen mass below the surface.' Yet they are more powerful than behaviors seen 'above the surface.'"

"What's another step to achieve your desired outcome?" Toni asked, returning from a short break.

Jim thought for a minute before answering. "I'm guessing it has something to do with having values that support collaborative leadership."

"Spot-on, Jim. Values are closely linked to underlying assumptions. A good example is trust—that is to say, a belief in the competence, reliability, and good intentions of others. When coaching others, I typically combine the ideas of underlying assumptions and values since they are so tightly linked." Walking to the whiteboard, Toni wrote:

Underlying Assumptions → Values → Behaviors

"Underlying assumptions shape values and, eventually, influence behaviors," Toni said.

"So positive underlying assumptions about people and their potential, for example, may lead to trust as a value that allows a manager to behave, say, in a delegating manner. Correct?"

Smiling, Toni paused before clarifying. "Not quite. Keep in mind that effective delegation requires that the person being tasked with a job or challenge is competent and has, if necessary, been trained to successfully perform the task. For example, you would not delegate the task of building a website to someone who has not been trained to do that. That's the caveat when it comes to delegation."

Jim nodded. "I can see how the dots are starting to connect here. In my case, for example, your coaching presence has allowed Brett to delegate the task of developing my collaborative leadership skills. Otherwise, I would be 'up a creek without a paddle,' as they say!"

"Well said, Jim."

So far, Toni was pleased with Jim's commitment to developing his self-awareness. His success to become a collaborative leader was tied directly to this challenge. She had seen numerous managers over the course of her career—as both a senior-level manager and a leader coach—fail because they lacked self-awareness. And the research supported her experience as well.

———

"Are you ready to talk some more about what you need to learn in order to become a collaborative leader?" Toni asked, returning from lunch.

"You bet."

Toni smiled. She knew that Jim would be eager to learn how he and his team could begin to collaborate. "The plan is to introduce you to a platform I use with clients to teach them how to effectively collaborate to produce win-win outcomes."

"Sounds really interesting, Toni."

"Jim, as you recall from earlier conversations, collaboration is part mind-set, part skill set."

"Yes, I'm tracking..."

"Applying a collaborative mind-set calls for using several novel team principles. As we discussed earlier, these principles are adapted from the game of soccer and mirror a team's behaviors and actions on the field. I also like to refer to these as *governing* principles as well because they help frame, or shape, individual and team decisions." Toni walked back to the whiteboard and began to write on it. "Here's one example," she said.

TEAM PRINCIPLE

Coach Teams To Respond To Changing Conditions On Their Own

Toni continued. "Again, when applied, these principles help to shape the choices your team makes when it comes to determining which essential competencies to use in a given situation. Because they affect team behaviors—and, ultimately, habits and team norms—the ability to make the right choices is critical to team success."

"When you talk about competencies, you're referring to skill set?"

"Good point, Jim!" Toni picked up her marker and headed to the whiteboard again.

Team Principles → Essential Competencies → Behaviors → Habits/Team Norms

Jim nodded. "I can understand why it's important to develop mind-set before skill set. And I'm starting to see why it's important to align these in a productive way."

"Without these principles, the team's actions and their application of competencies and various tools will be limited," Toni said, returning to her chair.

"Perfect. Let's keep it going," Jim said, excited to learn more.

Toni smiled. "When the principles and essential competencies are combined, they form the platform I mentioned earlier. This gets embedded in the team's charter. We'll talk more about your team's charter later. For now, we want to stay focused on the principles and the competencies."

"OK, I think I understand how these pieces fit together. But I do have a question regarding the underlying assumptions we talked about earlier. Where do they fit?"

"They certainly fit in." Walking back to the whiteboard, Toni began to write again.

> # Underlying Assumptions +
> # Team Principles + Essential Competencies +
> # Behaviors = Habits/Team Norms

"So, positive underlying assumptions about people and their potential, leveraged with the principles and competencies, help to produce behaviors, habits, and team norms that support team collaboration, which leads to outstanding team results," Jim said, pointing to the whiteboard.

"Precisely. Keep in mind, the essential competencies are aligned with the principles. That's why I said earlier that these principles help shape decisions regarding the specific competencies to employ in any given situation."

Jim walked into the house and was greeted by his wife and kids. "How was your day?" Diane asked.

"Interesting. I learned a few new things about the importance of connections."

"When you say connections, you mean relationships?"

"Good guess," Jim said, forcing a smile from his wife. "It's a long story. I'll tell you more after the kids go to bed."

7

STRANGER IN A STRANGE PLACE

T oni knew from her own experience that building self-awareness is a journey requiring Jim's buy-in and total commitment. She also knew that Jim was apprehensive about the idea of leading a team scattered around the globe. Managing people at all, much less people with cultural differences, made for a completely new set of challenges for him. On top of that, Brett was asking him to learn a new operating platform for developing team collaboration.

Managing change can be unnerving, to say the least. It takes courage. *Easier said than done*, Toni reminded herself. But Jim could not afford to be reluctant to learn and grow. Developing self-awareness was critical to his success. Although he may feel like a stranger in a strange place as he began his journey, the idea of failing in his new job was not an option she wanted to entertain.

———

"Where do you get your energy, Jim?" Toni asked, quickly starting their next coaching session.

"I'm not sure what you mean, Toni."

"OK, let me clarify. Do you prefer to get energy from yourself or from others?"

STRANGER IN A STRANGE PLACE

"I've always preferred to work alone, so that probably means I get energy from myself. It's one of the reasons I became a technician."

"Fair enough, Jim. Let me ask, how do you prefer to gather, or take in, information? With your intuition or with your senses? Intuition here can mean your gut."

"I think I can say that I prefer my senses. My focus has always been on what works now, if you know what I mean. That was the way it worked in my military job and as a lead tech before I was promoted."

Toni nodded. "OK, then, next question. How do you prefer to make decisions? With your head or with your heart?"

Jim smiled. "That's an easy one to answer. I think I've always had a talent for analyzing a problem or situation, especially if it's a technical issue dealing with logical choices and outcomes."

"Good. One final question. How do you prefer to go about your work—and life, for that matter? Do you prefer a structured situation? Or do you like to keep things 'open-ended,' as they say?"

"That's another easy one to answer. I prefer planning things both at work and at home."

"Great, Jim. Thanks for answering these four questions."

"What's the purpose behind the questions?"

"I was waiting for that question!" They both laughed.

"To answer *your* question. I use these questions to get a snapshot of who you are—that is, your personality."

Jim nodded.

"There's a survey I have clients complete confirming what I just asked you. It's called the Myers-Briggs Type Indicator®, or MBTI®. I will have you complete this survey in the future, but for now, this works to get us started."

As much as Toni valued the application of various surveys and assessments, as a coach she preferred to ask clients questions—especially in the beginning of an engagement. She often found this to be a good way to build a relationship with her clients. For her to be successful in working with Jim, Toni knew she would need to initially focus on relationship building and delve into technology and tools such as the MBTI later. However, she reasoned, there was no harm in giving Jim a little preview of what was to come.

Toni continued. "The answers you provided tell me some things about your personality—that is, your natural preferences when it comes to communicating, taking in information, making decisions, and organizing work. Based on what you told me, you could be someone with an MBTI profile described as an ISTJ."

Jim said nothing.

Toni pushed on. "Each letter represents a way to describe your *preferences*, and they are used in combination to produce what is called your MBTI profile. The letter I stands for introversion and is tied to the question I asked about your energy; S stands for sensing and is tied to how you gather information; T stands for thinking and is connected to how you make decisions; and J stands for judging—but not in the sense of judging others. It's connected to how much structure or organization you prefer in your work and life."

"Wow, that's a lot to grasp at one time!" Jim exclaimed, leaning back in his chair.

"I agree," Toni said, hoping to confirm that Jim was OK with this feedback before continuing. "Introverted, sensing, thinking, judging—does that sound like you?"

Jim pondered over Toni's feedback before responding, "I think it's a close fit."

"OK, then, we will plan to continue building your understanding of the MBTI in future coaching sessions."

"I'm glad you've got it figured out."

"For sure, Jim. That's one of the benefits of having a coach who's been trained and certified to use this tool."

Again, Jim nodded.

Toni continued with her coaching. "Obviously, we all have a personality that affects how we behave. Understanding that is all part of building your self-awareness and emotional intelligence as a leader."

"Can you give me an example?"

"You bet, Jim. As an ISTJ type, you would be described as a detail-oriented person. If that fits, then most likely your focus in your new leadership role will be on execution. This tendency is especially true for most new leaders with your MBTI profile who are just starting their development."

Again, Jim paused to let it all sink in. "It's sort of my default option, is what I'm hearing you say, Toni."

"Exactly."

They both smiled.

"It's important to understand that there are other descriptors of positive and negative behaviors used to describe your type. Again, we'll be talking about all of that later, once we build your understanding of MBTI. For now, here's an article that talks about introversion—the 'I' in your MBTI profile—that will help you understand the unique gifts you bring as an introvert that can be used to support your quest to become a collaborative leader."

Jim nodded.

"One last thing is to recognize that a team has a personality as well. The MBTI will come into play to help develop your team's emotional intelligence, or EQ—emotional quotient—as it's called. We'll plan to cover this later as well."

————

"Looks like you're deep in thought," Diane said after Jim walked into the house that evening.

"Sort of, I guess."

"What's up?"

"Just thinking about what I learned today about my personality."

"Do you want to talk about it?"

"No, at least not yet. I've got an article Toni asked me to read. I want to do that and have a chance to digest it before I say anything."

Diane nodded as Jim headed to the kitchen to grab a soda.

8

LAYING THE FOUNDATION

Jim sat at his desk and reflected on what he'd learned by reading the article Toni had given him. He now understood the meaning of the term, introversion, which Toni used to describe, in part, his personality type. Glancing around, he saw Toni approaching his office. "I read the article you gave me," he said, excited to share his feedback. "It made sense."

"That's great to hear, Jim. Keep in mind, however, that your personality type describes how you prefer to use your mind and your potential for development. It doesn't necessarily dictate your behavior, if you know what I mean."

Jim nodded.

Toni sensed an opportunity to push on. "You can't hide behind your ISJT profile, especially when it comes to how you act."

Holding his breath, Jim paused to let Toni's words sink in. "I know I can't—especially when it comes to communication."

"Glad to see you've made the connection."

Jim got up from his desk and walked over to close his office door. "The article also mentioned blind spots—something about reducing blind spots, as I recall. Can you help me understand that?"

"The term 'blind spot' is used to describe a lack of awareness you may have in regard to things around you; things that others are quite aware of."

"What do you mean?"

"If we're talking about communication, for example, it could be verbal cues, mannerisms, how you say things, and your style in relating to others."

"So, you're saying these things, or blind spots, can interfere with my success at communicating if I'm not aware of them. Correct?"

"Spot-on, Jim. If we are insensitive to our own behavior and what it may signal to others, it can be quite surprising and disconcerting to see that our attempts to communicate aren't very successful."

"Sounds like we're talking about one's credibility as a leader."

"Absolutely. Again, it's all about developing self-awareness. The endgame is to identify and reduce blind spots that can derail or interfere with your performance as a team leader. This includes understanding that a strength can become a weakness if it's overused."

"What's the best way to do that?"

"Glad you asked, Jim. If we are talking about developing emotional intelligence, for example, I use an EQ model to help identify blind spots. This model has been used by coaches and leaders for some time now."

"Sounds interesting."

"Let me pull up the model on my laptop," Toni said, grabbing her computer. "I will send this to you later today."

"Thanks."

"Here it is."

Jim leaned over to catch a glance.

"As you can see, there are four boxes, or domains, described as self-awareness, social awareness, self-management, and relationship management. Inside each domain is a list of competencies. Based on research, the self-awareness box is shaded to illustrate that it's a necessary underpinning of both social awareness and self-management."

"I can see that."

"Decades of research now point to EQ as the critical factor that sets high-performing leaders apart from others," Toni pointed out.

"When you say high-performing leaders, does that include collaborative leaders?"

"Absolutely!"

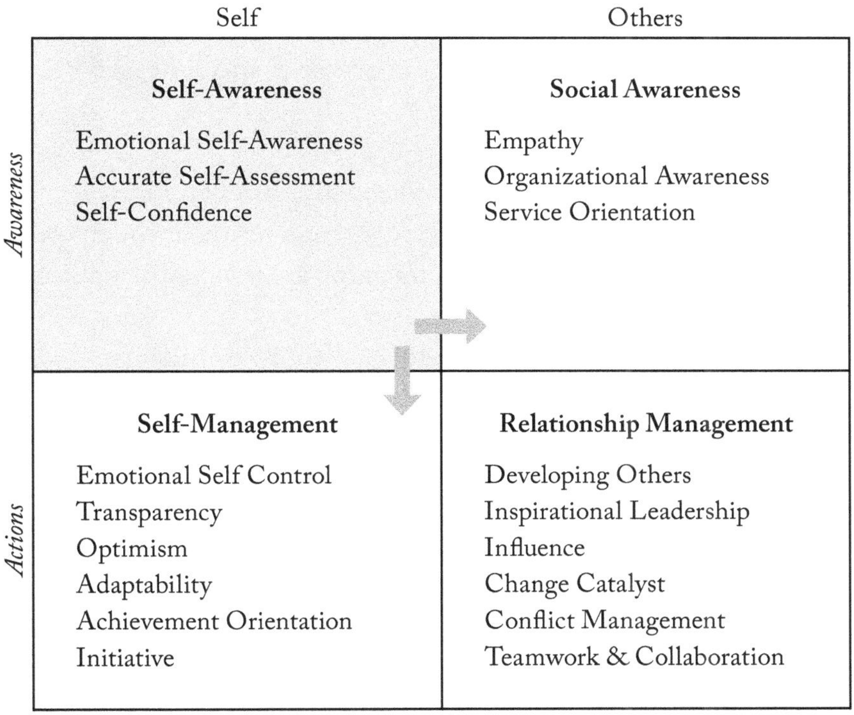

Self	Others
Self-Awareness Emotional Self-Awareness Accurate Self-Assessment Self-Confidence	**Social Awareness** Empathy Organizational Awareness Service Orientation
Self-Management Emotional Self Control Transparency Optimism Adaptability Achievement Orientation Initiative	**Relationship Management** Developing Others Inspirational Leadership Influence Change Catalyst Conflict Management Teamwork & Collaboration

Awareness (left side, top row) · *Actions* (left side, bottom row)

"Looks challenging," Jim said, quickly scanning the model.

"It looks overwhelming at first glance. The key is to manage it using a 360° survey tool to get honest feedback from people in your network on your strengths and weaknesses, eventually targeting selected competencies for development."

Jim nodded. "I've heard of this tool, but I've never used it."

"It's a very useful tool. But it can be threatening to some people."

"How so?"

"It may challenge your self-perception, especially if it's your first time using this tool."

Jim was curious. "Please tell me more, Toni."

"We know the goal is to increase self-awareness. When you take on a leadership role, it's important to recognize that *others'* perception of your leadership style is more important than *your* perception of your leadership style. Make sense?"

"Go ahead, say more."

"A big part of your transition to becoming a collaborative leader is acknowledging that you get productivity and results through others. That's why delegating and communicating are two key competencies to develop in the future."

Jim swallowed before responding to Toni's comments. "Sounds like I have to reinvent myself," he said, wincing slightly.

Toni paused before answering. "That's one way to describe it, Jim. As a new leader, your transition includes letting go of things like long-held values and assumptions that support nonproductive behaviors."

"Any examples?"

"In your case, several behaviors to be on the lookout for include a tendency to overcontrol, to be inflexible, and to be judgmental or critical of others, just to name a few. These can all be products of holding onto old, unproductive values or assumptions."

"I can relate."

Toni knew that her coaching challenge would be centered on Jim admitting his vulnerability as he loosened his psychological grip on the qualities that had made him successful as a technical expert. However, his new role as a leader demanded new skills and attributes. Jim's transition would require both learning agility and a huge leap of faith, as she liked to describe it. Moving from being a technical expert who focused on technical problems to being a leader who focused on people problems was a new game Jim would need to learn and play.

"Again, this can be a tough psychological transition to manage," Toni added.

"I think I understand what you're saying. This sounds like what I experienced when I went into the military, if you know what I mean."

Toni was somewhat relieved by Jim's reaction to this discussion. "There is some good news here, Jim. You want to retain your technical expertise because it helps you generate personal power that can be used to leverage your leadership agenda with the team. We'll talk more about personal power later."

Jim nodded.

"OK, then," Toni explained, "down the road—after you've been in your role for, say, four to six months—you can complete a 360° survey."

"I guess that makes sense. But what happens between now and then?"

Toni knew the value of completing a 360° survey. Once everyone on his team had been working together for a while, an assessment such as this would help Jim identify any blind spots he had about his own behavior—behavior that, by then, would be quite apparent to his team. The key, Toni knew, was for Jim to develop a receptive attitude and encourage people to give him honest feedback. Based on his MBTI profile, she suspected that Jim may have, among others, a blind spot associated with his analytical nature and its tendency to inadvertently stifle creativity. Obviously, that would not be good when it comes to innovation.

PART 3

Collaborative Leader Coaching Essentials

9

CRACK THE CODE

Toni walked into the conference room, eager to meet with Jim and Brett. On the whiteboard she wrote down the team principles she planned to review with them.

"You know that a collaborative mind-set is made up of several novel principles," she said after they'd arrived and everyone had settled in for their meeting.

Jim nodded while Brett sat quietly, taking in Toni's words.

"What you may not realize," she continued, "is how they support the shift from an authoritarian leadership style to a collaborative leadership style. The former style promotes dependency while the latter promotes interdependency. Obviously, this a far better fit for today's global business world where teams and team-based applications continue to grow."

"Sounds like a real shift in philosophy when you say it that way," Jim said.

"It's definitely a marked departure from traditional thinking and ways of operating. That's why I asked you earlier if we could include Brett in our work together today."

"Appreciate the invite," Brett said, jumping in. "I agree that it's important to understand the shift so I can support Jim and others as needed in the company."

"Brett, it's good to have you here," Toni said. "As you both know, these principles are adapted from the game of soccer and mirror the team's behaviors and actions on the field. Without them, your team's application of tools will be limited."

"Which is why you said earlier that it's important to develop the appropriate mind-set *before* you work on acquiring the needed skill set," Jim offered.

"Yes. In fact, developing mind-set before skill set is the key to unlocking the collaboration code," Toni declared emphatically.

Jim nodded. "Exactly."

Walking up to the whiteboard, Toni pointed to what she had written earlier.

TEAM PRINCIPLES

- Focus On Team, Not Position

- Understand That Everyone Can Play

- Embrace Diversity

- Rely On Each Other

- Promote Individual & Team Values

- Seek Out Skillful, Adaptable Players

- Charge The Team To Perform The Work

- Empower Players To Win

- Coach Teams To Respond To Changing Conditions On Their Own

- Develop Partners On The Field

- Achieve Cross-Cultural Agility

"It's also important to understand that I've listed these principles in no particular order and they all need to be in play all the time for your team to effectively collaborate."

Reflecting on what he'd just heard, Jim asked, "What do these principles really mean when applied?"

"Good question, Jim. They help to establish a shared approach to managing the team's actions and behaviors."

Jim nodded.

"Jim, say you're leading a team that's working on a project," Toni said. "Your project is one-third complete. Your client proposes a change to the project. While the proposed change has merit, it would expand the project's scope beyond its original parameters. Most likely, this would delay the project's completion date and exceed budget projections. Keep in mind that you're dealing with a long-term client."

"So, the question for Jim is how to integrate the client's proposed change in the project?" Brett offered.

"Exactly. What say you, Jim?"

"Wow. That's a lot to deal with," Jim said, getting up from his chair and walking across the conference room to stretch his legs—and think. Damn! The last thing he wanted was to embarrass himself in front of Brett. He held his breath and stared at the whiteboard, hoping the right answer would come to him.

"Jim, what do you think your decision will reveal about you, if you're the team leader in this scenario?" Toni finally asked.

Jim sat down. "Perhaps something about the team leader's mind-set."

"Spot-on, Jim. If you've worked on a project with any customer in the past, you'll recognize the phrase 'wouldn't it be great if.' This is a sure sign that the project's scope is going to be challenged. A change introduced now could delay the project and add cost."

"So, Jim's faced with a few choices," Brett added.

"Correct. If we limit his choices either to holding a team meeting to decide how to proceed or to simply tell the client that your team will deliver on the client's request, which option would you choose?"

Jim grabbed his bottle of water and took a sip. "The first choice looks like a more inclusive option. If that's the case, then it's a way to demonstrate a collaborative mind-set, I'm guessing."

"Correct again, Jim," Toni said. She walked back to the whiteboard and wrote out this key principle.

TEAM PRINCIPLE

Coach Teams To Respond To Changing Conditions On Their Own

"As you can see, the first choice promotes this operating principle. However, it may be the riskier option if time is a concern."

"What about the second choice?" Jim asked.

"Obviously, this choice puts your client first," Toni said, sitting down. "That's not all bad, but it may upset your team. This may place the project's key performance indicators—such as quality, schedule, and budget—at risk."

Jim nodded and leaned back in his chair. "I see what you mean."

Brett was curious. "Toni, are other principles in play here?"

"Great question, Brett. The answer is yes. In this example, there are other principles in play, but this is the key, or leading, principle used to demonstrate a collaborative mind-set."

"Toni, do you have any other way to help describe each competency when applied?" Jim asked.

"Yes. For each competency in the platform, there's a description," Toni said, leaning over to hand Jim and Brett a one-page document.

"Perfect," Jim said, glancing over at Brett. "This is helpful."

"As you can see," Toni continued, "the description of each principle is brief, straightforward, and easy to understand. Again, your challenge is to apply these in the course of your team's work—keeping in mind that, to greater or lesser degrees, they are all in play, or operational, all the time."

Team Principles

Focus On Team, Not Position. Addresses the need to focus on results that can be produced when all team members effectively interact on the business field.

Understand That Everyone Can Play. Recognizes that technology is the great enabler that allows people everywhere to collaborate.

Embrace Diversity. Represents a prerequisite for partnering in global business, serves as a springboard for establishing trust, and brings strength to teams.

Rely On Each Other. Reinforces the team orientation, minimizes the silo mind-set, recognizes interdependency among team members, and supports genuine collaboration.

Promote Both Individual and Team Values. Deals with managing both values in a never-ending cycle to help ensure that the process employed to produce team results is working,

Seek Out Skillful, Adaptable Players. Promotes the need for flexibility when managing change, requires people and teams who can quickly assimilate and employ new skills and information, and recognizes that multiple skills are needed to perform effectively.

Charge The Team To Perform The Work. Recognizes the self-directed nature of the team charged with accomplishing the task or challenge and recognizes that the team is responsible for its own performance.

Empower Players To Win. Speaks to the commitment required to develop all team members and to provide continuous feedback with the goal of helping and encouraging them to make better decisions.

Coach Teams To Respond To Changing Conditions On Their Own. Reinforces the need to coach people on teams to manage their own performance in real-time under changing conditions for the purpose of producing positive results.

Develop Partners On The Field. Recognizes that all players on the business field are to be viewed as leaders and promotes the recognition of every opportunity as a leadership development step.

Achieve Cross-Cultural Agility. Calls for understanding the pivotal nature of relationships—and relationship building—to achieve positive results across cultures.

Toni continued. "It's the combination of all these principles that describes a collaborative mind-set. Without this understanding and application, the principles fail to support team collaboration."

"Is that why you said earlier that people could not switch mind-sets on demand, like flipping a switch?" Brett asked.

"Yes, Brett. That's what makes this both an operational and a developmental challenge. But the good news is that a collaborative mind-set can be learned."

"Does skill set come into play here?" Brett asked.

"For sure, Brett said. Let's hold that question for now, though, if that's OK. We'll address it soon."

Later that day, Brett rejoined Jim and Toni to pick up their discussion from the morning session. Now that he had a better understanding of how a collaborative mind-set played out, he was looking forward to hearing about the application of a collaborative skill set.

"Brett, you asked earlier about skill set," Toni pointed out.

Brett nodded.

Pointing to the whiteboard, Toni said, "holding a team meeting to decide how to proceed is the first option, and it promotes this principle:

Coach Teams To Respond To Changing Conditions On Their Own

"There are three essential competencies aligned with this principle that come into play to describe skill set," Toni continued.

THREE ESSENTIAL COMPETENCIES

- Adaptability
- Problem Solving & Decision Making
- Communication

"In our example, the team's purpose for collaborating is to drive creative, real-time problem solving and to entertain the possibility of changing direction. This also requires communication."

Jumping in, Jim said, "I see what you mean."

"The team's ability to be successful is directly related to its commitment to develop these competencies, along with its commitment to use them at work," Toni said.

"What you're saying, Toni," Brett remarked, "is that, combined, these three essential competencies provide the team the best opportunity to target behaviors that will fulfill the client's request. Correct?"

"For sure, Brett," Toni said, returning to the whiteboard. "Now, with each competency in the framework, we describe a list of behaviors to help people understand the meaning of the competency. For example, here's what it looks like for the competency of adaptability."

ADAPTABILITY BEHAVIORS

- Flexible & Open to New Ideas
- Quick to Adapt to New and Changing Situations
- Adept at Employing Change Management Techniques
- Comfortable with Ambiguity

Experience taught Toni that it was important to describe the competencies in behavioral terms for people to understand their full meaning.

"I know I sound like a broken record, but you've really got this mapped out in a very user-friendly way," Jim exclaimed.

"Thanks. This will go a long way toward helping your team develop and apply all the competencies listed in the platform," Toni said.*

Everyone paused to let Toni's feedback sink in.

"Toni, thanks for taking the time to answer my question from this morning," Brett said. "This was helpful."

Jim nodded in agreement.

"Glad to hear that," Toni said. "What was most useful part for each of you?"

"For me," Brett replied, "this example shows how competencies overlap and build on each other depending on the situation."

"And for me," Jim said, "it reinforces the need to have multiple competencies developed and available in the team's inventory in order for the team to be effective."

"Here's a question often comes up when I'm coaching clients on this platform's application," Toni said, "and it deals with managing team conflict: would the team be successful if conflict surfaced in its decision-making process? The answer comes from understanding that these three essential competencies may not be the only competencies that come into play in any particular situation. The competency, conflict management, for example, could be applied, if needed. Although it's not one of the 'big three' I mentioned earlier, it would become a valuable competency to focus on if conflict surfaced as part of the team's decision-making process."

"Awesome!" Jim replied.

————

Brett was encouraged, to say the least, after sitting through today's session with Toni and Jim. The company's recent acquisition had provided a timely opportunity to invest in new processes and projects, and both the coaching and the management ideas Toni brought to

* A complete list of all the competencies included in the operating platform is found in the Appendix.

the table seemed to be winning examples of these. Although the operating platform introduced by Toni was also new to him, he embraced its application inside his department. He believed it could be a blueprint for the company; for that reason, he wanted to fully understand its application. Since he worked in a risk-taking culture, he was confident that, if he could get the rest of the upper management team on board, his company's commitment to using Toni's platform would be strong. He planned to share what he'd learned with the senior leadership team soon.

10

PARTNERS
OR PRISONERS?

"What's on your mind?" Toni asked Jim, wondering how he was feeling about his team's development.

"I'd like to talk about setting up a goal for my team to develop the essential competencies in the platform."

Toni was curious. "What are you thinking?"

"One idea is to ask everyone on the team to start working on a few competencies I think are important. That way it feels like we're all on the same page."

"Sort of a top-down approach, is what I'm hearing."

"Yeah, that's one way to describe it," Jim said, clearing his throat.

"Would you like any suggestions from me?"

"Sure."

"I thought you would," Toni said, popping open her laptop. "These are the essential competencies aligned with the principles in our platform. Keep in mind, your ability to successfully apply these, as individuals or as a team, is tied to being mindful of which competencies are aligned with each of the principles."

Team Principles	Essential Competencies
Focus On Team, Not Position	Adaptability, Learning Agility
Understand That Everyone Can Play	Drive & Energy, Initiative, Functional/Technical Expertise
Embrace Diversity	Global Mind-Set, Relationship Building
Rely On Each Other	Relationship Building, Team Management, Team Player
Promote Both Individual & Team Values	Global Mind-Set, Integrity, Relationship Building
Seek Out Skillful, Adaptable Players	Adaptability, Learning Agility, Organizing & Planning
Charge The Team To Perform the Work	Customer Orientation, Results Orientation, Visioning
Empower Players To Win	Problem Solving & Decision Making, Risk Taking
Coach Teams To Respond To Changing Conditions On Their Own	Adaptability, Problem Solving & Decision Making, Communicativeness
Develop Partners On The Field	Communicativeness, Coaching, Delegation, Influence, Relationship Building
Achieve Cross-Cultural Agility	Global Mind-Set, Learning Agility, Relationship Building, Self-Objectivity

Toni knew that organizational development experts would describe this as the 'alignment' of principles, processes, people, and other elements of a dynamic entity or situation. She believed such an alignment, played out across all structures and systems inside an organization, would establish a competitive advantage for all stake-holders. It reminded her of Toyota and its 'Toyota Way' of managing.

"Any questions so far?" Toni asked, looking at Jim.

Jim scanned the handout. "Not yet. But I have a couple of observations to share as I look this over. First, it looks like relationship building shows up frequently in many of the team principles. Second, it looks like several competencies, including adaptability and learning agility, deal with the need to be responsive to changing demands and scenarios."

Toni nodded. "Good observations, Jim. Adaptability, which I often refer to as *change agility*, and relationship building are two of the most important competencies."

Jim continued to scan the handout.

"Typically, we asked people to complete a 360° survey to determine where they stand on all the essential competencies," Toni explained.

"You want to identify strengths and weaknesses."

"Yes. Since you and your team are so new, it doesn't make sense to do that right now."

"Another case of hurry up and wait!"

"Afraid so, Jim. A good alternative you can do now, however, is to have everyone on your team complete self-assessments to rate their proficiency levels on all the essential competencies in the operating platform. It's a quick, straightforward exercise that will help to personalize their development."

"And from there we can identify strengths and weaknesses for each person."

"Exactly. It should lead to higher commitment to the team's development process. What say you about that idea?"

"I like it. It's definitely not a top-down approach, but more participative."

Becoming proficient in targeted competencies, Toni believed, was key to collaboration. Jim needed to find every opportunity to **develop partners on the field** who were responsive to building both task and team competence, generating the team synergy to produce results. The consequences of failing to accomplish this goal were not positive. Toni knew that, for example, low-level engagement on the part of employees could not always be overcome—and it was most commonly found in organizations that failed to treat people as valued resources whose development was a priority. Although this company had begun to dramatically improve the way in which it viewed and treated its employees, it was possible that Jim might have to replace one or more team members who either couldn't or wouldn't commit to the firm's new development process.

"OK, Jim, I will follow up with you tomorrow to get your team's self-assessments started. Anything else?"

"So, with this platform's application," Jim said, picking his words carefully, "it looks like we're setting expectations for people and the team. Right?"

"Yes. That's one way to describe it. And it also gets us back to looking at your team's charter and how it's used to establish performance expectations in the form of team norms."

"Makes sense so far, Toni."

"Jim, the idea of teaching your people a new range of competencies may appear challenging—at least in the beginning. It takes time, but it's not complicated."

"I think that, once we get comfortable with the language of competency development, we should be fine," Jim offered.

"Good point, Jim. Keep in mind, development usually includes workshops, reading, special assignments, job rotation, and the like."

"And don't forget your coaching!" Jim said, forcing a smile from Toni.

"Definitely! As your coach, my job is to build your commitment for learning new competencies before moving on to developing proficiencies or skills. The good news—you already have proficiencies in many of these competencies. The same holds true for people on your team."

Toni felt confident that the decision to invest in developing his team was set in Jim's mind. This would include Jim requiring everyone on the team to **function as a leader**—and viewing every opportunity to work with his people as a **leadership development step**.

————

Jim walked into the house late that evening. "You look tired," Diane said.

Wincing slightly, Jim said, "Yeah, it's been busy. Lots going on. And it's very challenging. But I'm making progress, even though it feels like it's slow.

"That's encouraging to hear."

"How are the kids doing?" Jim asked, heading off to see if they were asleep.

11

LEADER AS COACH

Jim and Toni spent the entire afternoon preparing for Jim's first coaching session. After sharing some coaching tips, Toni led Jim through a series of role-plays, with Jim acting as coach and Toni as client. The role-playing sessions were helpful, but he quickly learned how ill-prepared he was to effectively coach people. More than ever, he really appreciated Toni's coaching skills.

––––––––

Driving to his office the following morning, all Jim could think about was coaching. He'd scheduled a team meeting at nine to deal with an issue that recently surfaced. Because Toni had a conflict, he was on his own to work with the team and provide coaching, if needed.

Jim had a good relationship with his people. Toni believed that would give him the freedom to practice his coaching, make mistakes, and move on quickly. Yet he had this nagging worry about his ability to shift roles as needed to coach his team.

Jim grabbed a cup of coffee and made his way to the conference room to meet his team. "What's up?" Jim asked, glancing at his four local IT specialists. They looked nervous. Andy, in particular, seemed on the verge of a meltdown.

"We've discovered a skills gap," Andy said, throwing his hands into the air, "and unless you can fix this now, we just don't see how we can be expected to handle our new project!"

Jim quickly surveyed the other IT specialists. They looked concerned, but no one else seemed to be panicking. Jim knew that Andy was the emotional member of the team. Did everybody actually think the project was doomed before it had started!

Jim calmly sat down and asked the team to fill him in on the problem with the project they were about to begin. As it turned out, the IT specialists had discovered that a highly technical skill would be required to effectively complete this project—one the team did not possess. Delays in starting the project were not acceptable, but trying to get by without the skill was risky.

"What can be done to fill the gap?" Andy wanted to know.

———

"How was your doctor's visit?" Jim asked Toni when she popped-in the office to catch up with him later that day.

"Just routine. How did your meeting go this morning?"

Choosing his words carefully, Jim said, "This team coaching role has me concerned."

"Tell me more."

Jim swallowed before answering. "Worried, I guess."

"Before we talk about your coaching experience this morning, tell me what you're feeling."

"My comfort level is not very high. I'm a little scared," he admitted.

Toni continued to probe for Jim's benefit. "OK, not surprising. What else?"

Jim rolled up his sleeves. "I feel like it's several things, like time management and lack of training. And not wanting to screw up—just to name a few!" he blurted out.

"That's good feedback. We can tackle all of this down the road. Trust me."

Nodding, Jim smiled, trying to settle his emotions while paying attention to Toni.

Toni could sense that Jim was not at ease. She knew from experience that coaching was not for everyone. Yet she was convinced that Jim's mind-set would go a long way to help him succeed. After all, the success of coaching depended on more than just a skill set. In addition, it was highly dependent on a coaching mind-set.

"Tell me what worked for you this morning in coaching the team."

Jim pulled a small notebook out of his desk. "Let me check my notes." He slowly turned a few pages before responding to Toni's question. "The biggest takeaway was the fact that we were able to come up with an internal solution to our challenge. It took a while, but the team recommended that Jill gets a chance to develop her technical skills to fill the gap. She has an interest in developing this technical skill, so it's a good fit. She's excited."

"That's great. Any downside to the team's solution?"

"It will take her some added time and some help from the rest of the team. But they can make it work."

"Sounds like you applied the principle **seek out skillful, adaptable players** to your team's solution."

"Good point. That and the principle **rely on each other** were both in play here," Jim offered.

———

After a short break, Jim and Toni resumed their discussion. "Let's flip things and talk about what didn't work well for you this morning," suggested Toni.

Jim began turning pages in his notebook. "I struggled with Andy's emotions. I believe others did as well."

Toni nodded. "Say more."

"Perhaps he was not aware of his behavior on the team. I tried a few times to redirect him, but I wasn't all that successful, if you know what I mean."

"So, you had to deal with conflict. How was that experience?"

"Andy wanted to hire an outside contractor to fill the skills gap," Jim said, leaning back in his chair. "He argued that it would be the quickest way to deal with the issue. The others didn't like his idea. They were concerned with the time it may take to recruit someone with the appropriate skill set, along with the potential disruption to the integrity of the team."

"How did you resolve the conflict?"

"The decision was made to go with the team's consensus after I suggested this option."

"Was Andy OK with that?"

"I guess. Only time will tell, as they say."

"OK," Toni said, pondering for the moment. "This is a good time to point out a couple of things to think about in coaching your team. First, most of your coaching will be focused on individual team members. This will give you a better chance of encouraging people to take personal responsibility and accountability for their actions."

"Please say more."

"Sure. A key task as the team's leader is to instill in each team member a sense of responsibility for the team's well-being. You can do this by making sure your team's norms are established and explicit so that people can practice them repeatedly."

"Any examples to share?"

"Sure. Interpersonal understanding, perspective taking, conflict resolution, and caring are a few norms that help build trust and a common commitment to goals."

"I can definitely relate to that after my experience this morning with Andy."

"Perfect. The other point worth mentioning here is centered on building the team's self-awareness. Obviously, this will take time, just as it does with individuals."

Jim nodded. "Are the team's competencies the same as those of an individual's?"

"Yes. That's the good news."

Toni pushed on. "We know the real difference between effective teams and ineffective teams lies in the team's emotional intelligence, or EQ. Teams have an EQ of their own; it's composed of everyone's individual EQ plus the EQ of the team as a collective."

"So, by working with individuals to develop their self-awareness, I have a better chance of developing the team's overall EQ effectiveness," Jim said, paraphrasing what he'd heard Toni say.

"Exactly. And with everyone contributing to the overall level of the team's EQ, as the team's leader you end up with more influence!"

"Makes sense. But how do I develop the team's self-awareness?"

"Good question, Jim. A few different assessment tools are available to begin the process of team member development. We're going to use the MBTI assessment. As you now know, this tool helps to provide a better understanding of one's own style, leading to acceptance and understanding of how team members are different in the way they work."

"I like that, Toni. Using the same tool will make it easier for me to develop my team."

"OK then, one last thing to mention today about coaching individuals on your team. After that, we'll shift gears and talk about team stuff."

Jim nodded.

"You know that performance expectations are typically expressed as goals."

"Yes."

"Your coaching comes in to help your people accomplish those goals. Here, we're primarily talking about improving their competencies or skills for achieving results. However, it may also include coaching to deal with their commitment, if necessary."

"This applies to coaching both individuals and the team?"

"Yes. And that's a good segue to talk about team coaching. Two good examples of what I mean by team coaching include managing the team's charter and managing team building," Toni said. "The first task is something we'll talk about tomorrow."

"OK."

Toni continued. "The second task deals with managing the changing nature of your team. Because teams are normally in flux, your task is to monitor the team's performance and adjust the way you manage the team in order to keep them focused. Your team will likely go through a series of identifiable stages of performance on a given task: forming, storming, norming, and performing. Your ability to use multiple styles to support your team's progression is critical to your success at being their 'leader as coach.' You would not use a directing style, for example, to manage your people and the team 100 percent of the time. That would not be effective in the long run."

"That's a lot to grasp," Jim said, making note of Toni's input.

"I agree. Developing flexibility in the way you lead others is a skill set that will take training and time. We will leave that task for another time and place."

"As long as it involves your coaching, Toni!" Jim said, reminding her of the value she added as a coach.

———

The following morning Toni and Jim resumed their conversation. So far, Jim's overall commitment to becoming a collaborative leader was high, although he did seem reluctant to serve in the role of 'leader as coach.' This was not an easy role to take on because it demanded his added commitment to develop his coaching competence or skill set. It was likely that, if Jim wanted to pursue this part of his learning journey in the future, he would need to seek out training from a bona fide coach training organization such as the one she'd attended. But that would come later in Jim's progression as a leader.

"Jim, yesterday I briefly mentioned the task of managing your team's charter. I've laid out the components in the charter using this handout to describe where to focus your coaching. Because there is only a limited number of components listed here, I've elected to call it a team mini-charter."

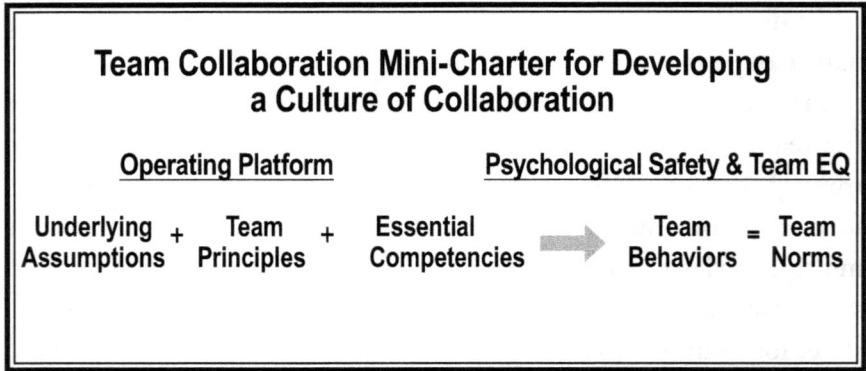

Team Collaboration Mini-Charter for Developing a Culture of Collaboration

Operating Platform   Psychological Safety & Team EQ

Underlying Assumptions + Team Principles + Essential Competencies ➡ Team Behaviors = Team Norms

---

"Typically, a team charter is described as a set of agreements that clearly describe what the team wants to accomplish, why it's important, and how the team will work together to achieve results," Toni explained. "Most team charters have components that describe vision, mission, purpose, values, norms, team member roles, key responsibility areas, team goals, communication strategies, decision-making authority and accountability, and available resources."

"Again, that's a lot to deal with."

"For sure, Jim. However, I've limited this discussion on the team's charter to the components that are critical to practicing team collaboration. This means that you and your team remain responsible for addressing the missing components in your team's charter, such as team mission."

Indeed, developing a team charter represents only a key piece of the larger framework needed for developing a culture of collaboration. Other components include HR systems and processes, compensation and rewards, and goal setting. She believed a collaborative mindset, established at the top of the organization and cascading down throughout the organization, would be the most significant part of a company's framework.

"Looks like you've got psychological safety covered well here," Jim pointed out.

"Glad you noticed, Jim. Our charter has three essential conditions to support this need: clear boundaries; a sense of meaning, urgency, and impact; and team competence. The first two conditions are covered in the principles and the third is covered in the competencies."

"I can see that *how* trumps *who* when it comes to the team's performance!"

Toni smiled. "Absolutely. How people work together is more important than who is on the team. When people are free to express themselves and take risks without feeling insecure or embarrassed, for example, they have increased psychological safety, which is to say that team trust is in place."

Oftentimes, Toni was asked by clients why the principles were needed. Her answer: to establish and sustain team trust. This was especially true for virtual teams such as Jim's, whose members were limited in their ability to use more traditional—and often, more social—ways to establish trust. The principles help provide a shared approach to describing expectations about how people would perform together.

PART 4

Team Collaboration Development Challenges

12

IT'S ALL IN THE GAME

"I think we all agree that everyone on the team should be on the same page when it comes to managing performance expectations," Toni said, sitting down to continue her coaching with Jim.

"No doubt, Toni. Last week I had a Zoom® meeting with the team. We had a great conversation about how to leverage the team's platform across all four global sales offices. This included acknowledging that soccer's metaphor gave us a unique way to connect as a team and perform in a consistent way."

"Perfect. Tell me more?"

"As you know, the sport of soccer represents a global language that people relate to and understand. We talked about how this can help us develop relationships and collaborate at each sales office."

Toni pondered this. It certainly stimulated her thinking about future possibilities regarding ways that each sales office could connect with their customers and stakeholders to develop a network of teams. "I like to describe this as **cross-cultural agility**," she said.

"I like that! Besides being another one of our principles, it ties-in well to the adaptability and learning agility competencies we talked about earlier."

"Good point, Jim."

Jim continued. "Carlos and his team in São Paulo believe it really gives them a vision of how they can work as a team not only in Brazil, but across our global network," Jim said emphatically.

"That's great feedback, Jim. Not only does it give them an organizing framework that's comprehensible across cultures, but it also will help establish a common bond and trust across each team's network."

Toni appreciated Jim's enthusiasm. She knew soccer was ingrained in the cultures of many countries around the world, including Brazil, and was part of their national character. She recalled when her old boss married his passion for soccer with his passion for leadership. His purpose was to introduce a new metaphor that resonated with people working across cultures to help them negotiate meaning, build rapport, and improve communication. That way, people could act on it in positive ways.

Both Toni and Jim sat silent for a moment before Toni said, "Another point worth making here is to realize that this will help your people establish a compelling purpose for generating the necessary passion and commitment to cocreate their future and perform as a real team that effectively collaborates."

Jim nodded, pondering Toni's feedback before responding. "I'm beginning to see what you mean. The powers of purpose and passion go a long way toward helping people achieve results. That was one of the lessons I learned in the military," he said with a twinkle in his eye.

"I agree wholeheartedly!"

They both smiled.

"The endgame is to have your team **operate in a self-directed way to perform the work that's needed to be done**. This may feel like a lofty goal. But your team can get there with the right leadership and coaching."

"Don't forget team development," Jim chided good-naturedly.

"Not to worry, Jim. That goes without saying."

"So how do we start the team development process to achieve this goal?"

"A good first step is to start providing as much context as possible for everyone on the team, including those in the field. The more context, the better."

"Can you elaborate, Toni?"

"Sure. Getting back to our metaphor—soccer is all about vision. For example, providing context means all players understand the big picture in order to function effectively, make decisions, and take risks as the flow of the game dictates," Toni explained. "Since it's played in a continuous way, players must respond to changing conditions on their own. The team's awareness of what's happening at any given moment is critical to its performance effectiveness."

"So, for my team, we need to find ways to share information, help them anticipate, and be responsive to stakeholder needs. Correct?"

"As a remote team leader, developing and implementing a communications plan is critical. Reaching out to both individuals and the team regularly, is going to be a top priority! That's why the essential competency, communicativeness, is ranked high in our team's platform."

"OK, what else?"

"One thing for you to learn is how to effectively delegate. This will benefit you and the team in many ways. For example, speed is critical to innovation, and your effective, timely delegation allows the team to respond to customer and stakeholder needs in an effective, timely way."

"So, you're saying it isn't enough to collaborate to innovate; I need to *delegate* to innovate as well."

"You've got it, Jim."

———

The next day, Jim made his way over to the product development office. He walked into the lab and found Kyle, one of his new IT specialists, with two members of the product development staff. Jim's mouth fell open when he heard Kyle and the others apparently arguing. On Monday he'd assigned Kyle to help troubleshoot a product glitch for a client. It needed to be accomplished by the following Monday. Jim walked over to the three, hoping to understand what was going on. The two product development people saw him coming and stopped talking. At that moment, Jim realized he needed to redirect Kyle.

Kyle said nothing as Jim pulled him aside and started to tell him what to do. The idea that Jim may be interfering with the group's performance never crossed his mind.

Later that day, sitting in the cafeteria, Jim overheard the same two people from the product development office talking about Jim's intervention with Kyle. They described it as badgering. One mentioned that Kyle had reacted as though he'd been scolded by an overcontrolling parent.

Walking back to his office after lunch, Jim pondered over what he'd just heard. Obviously, his actions had not been productive; he'd overreacted, to say the least. Jim reflected on what Toni said in an earlier coaching session about letting go of old, unproductive values and assumptions that support nonproductive behaviors, and he realized his tendency to overcontrol situations was one of them. Jim knew that he had to find Kyle and apologize.

––––––––

The following morning, Toni stopped by Jim's office unexpectedly. She'd left her laptop in his office. "Just came by to grab my laptop."

Jim pointed to the chair in the corner. "There you go."

Sensing that something might be troubling him, Toni remarked, "You look like you just lost your best friend. What's up?"

Jim paused before responding. "I guess I have to learn how to get out of the way."

"OK, that doesn't sound good. Tell me what's going on."

"I screwed up!"

After hearing Jim describe what had happened, Toni knew she couldn't turn back now. "Sounds like you're guilty of oversupervision. It's not a criminal offense," she said, trying to add some levity to the situation.

Jim smiled.

"One of the possible negative outcomes of ineffective delegation is the suppression of collaboration. We also call that oversupervising. The other possible negative outcome is called undersupervising, with delegation looking more like abdication, if you know what I mean."

"I can relate to that too," he responded immediately.

"At the end of the day, developing your competence to effectively delegate requires flexibility in how you lead others. This gets us back to the training program I mentioned the other day—the one I participated in many years ago—that teaches managers how to effectively delegate. We'll plan to get you scheduled for that program in the near future."

"Sounds good, Toni. Thanks."

Toni smiled. "Participants in that program found its lessons to be a resource that enabled them to function as increasingly knowledgeable and insightful leaders. It focused on learning how to adapt to employees' various and changing needs and to employ a variety of leadership styles to address them. This is critical to achieving success on the job."

Jim nodded, leaning back in his chair.

Toni knew that the ability to effectively delegate would be key to Jim's success. He would need to understand the value of delegating and embrace the idea of giving up some control in order to move from 'leader as expert' to a leader who **promotes 'shared' leadership** and who **empowers players to win.**

————

"Dan, thanks for meeting me for lunch," Jim said.

"No problem. This works well for me today. I've got a dental appointment just down the road in a couple of hours."

Jim nodded.

"How are things going?" Dan asked once they'd ordered their meals.

"Not bad. My IT people in the field, for example, have really embraced the metaphor of soccer."

"I'm not surprised. There's a reason people call it 'the beautiful game.'"

"Tell me more, Dan. I'm not familiar with that description."

"I believe it has something to do with the simplicity of the game. Soccer resonates with people everywhere because it's inspiring to see how people collaborate to produce winning outcomes."

"You're suggesting that it gives people hope?"

Dan thought about it for a minute. "That too," he said, nodding.

13

FAILING FAST

Winning in the game of innovation requires failing fast, Toni knew. Innovation is a product of the team's ability to collaborate across their network. It doesn't emanate from individuals on the team. The idea of failing fast must be embedded in a team's charter. Here, establishing team norms to support collaboration becomes the differentiator to ensure that the team's psychological safety remains intact.

"Jim, did you get a chance to watch the Women's World Cup soccer game over the weekend?" Toni asked on their way to grab some lunch.

"I did! Diane, the kids, and I went over to Dan's place to watch the game."

Toni smiled. "Great."

Jim nodded.

"I know you don't have a complete understanding of soccer. Any takeaways to share?"

"It's amazing to see how 'adaptable' the players were in moving the ball on the field."

"Absolutely. The game demands it. Being able to change quickly, assimilate new information on the run, and apply multiple skills are just a few of the key actions and behaviors. What else?"

"The women's team really practiced collaborative leadership, **relying on each other** to generate a high level of interdependence. In fact, that's the first thing I picked up after watching Real Madrid play on TV at Dan's house."

Toni nodded. "You just mentioned 'rely on each other,' which is one of our principles!"

Jim smiled. "See, the principles are already embedded in my vocabulary."

They both laughed.

"You mentioned before that Dan coaches soccer. Did he have any feedback from the game?"

"Dan pointed out that the team was constantly managing change. Plus, the players were not governed by their failures."

"He's right. As players collaborated on the field during the game, they were not successful on every play—and that's to be expected. A player might fail to maintain possession of the ball, complete a pass on-target to another player, make a tackle, or score a goal, but these actions are not viewed as failures. They are recognized as team behaviors that are part of the dynamic of team play throughout the game. But it's critical for players to move on to the next opportunity—quickly!"

Toni recognized there was not a hierarchy in place to interfered with the team's ability to collaborate and manage change. She also knew that many organizations were strapped with vertical hierarchies that would not work in a game like soccer—or in today's VUCA world—requiring everyone on the field to **function as a leader** to manage constant change effectively.

"It's interesting how teams that effectively collaborate—despite missteps or mistakes—find opportunities to be creative and succeed," Jim said.

"Glad you picked up on that."

Jim smiled.

Toni continued. "In soccer, players are continuously trying to innovative to score goals. Again, failing fast is embedded in the team's play to create even more opportunities to succeed."

"Failing fast?" Jim said, puzzled. "That's a new one for me."

"Because the game is played in a continuous manner, it's critical that players move on quickly after failing to complete a pass, for example. Responding to failure in a timely fashion leads to added opportunities to succeed. Make sense?"

"Yeah. I think I've got it."

"It's really no different than, say, the idea of embracing failure in our VUCA world, where innovation is critical to business growth," Toni explained. "This requires people on teams to collaborate and generate ideas in order to produce innovative solutions—much like soccer players generate game plays in order to score goals."

"So, if we want to succeed in the game of innovation, the concept of failing fast must be embedded in my team's charter."

"Absolutely."

"Collaborate to innovate!" Jim said emphatically.

"That places added importance on your team's charter and the need to make your operating platform produce and sustain psychological safety," cautioned Toni.

"Good point. That also places a premium on trust when it comes to effective collaboration. Without team trust, we would really fail to collaborate as a team. At best, we'd merely be coordinating or cooperating."

Toni nodded. "You have your work cut out for you as the team's leader. And it makes your role as 'leader as coach' very important."

Jim knew he was in a challenging situation. Yet he realized how fortunate he was to work in a company that had not been dragged kicking and screaming into the future. This included having a supportive supervisor who was willing to be an early adopter of team collaboration.

———

"We know the endgame is to effectively collaborate in order to innovate and grow the company," Toni said, as the two returned to their conversation that afternoon.

Jim nodded.

"What one thing stands in the way of being able to effectively play the innovation game?" Toni asked, hoping to stimulate Jim's thinking.

"Breaking down silos."

"For sure. Collaborating to innovate requires inclusion, and you can't get that when silos are interfering with the team's responsiveness and performance."

"Agree."

"Let's keep this going—what else stands in the way?"

"Capturing the ideas people bring to the table."

"Excellent answer, Jim! It's critical to **recognize and value team diversity**, including diversity of ideas."

"Isn't this one of our principles?"

"Glad you remembered. Being receptive to everyone's ideas is a very important part of promoting the team's psychological safety."

"Say more, Toni."

"The reality is, people may stay quiet for fear of embarrassment or even punishment if they've found that their ideas are rejected or are not recognized as valid input for the team's consideration."

"Good point. Thanks for clarifying that, Toni."

"We know diversity brings strength to teams in many ways, but the opportunities it provides to capture the ideas of a variety of people may be number one."

"So, we need diversity with inclusion to effectively collaborate to innovate."

"Absolutely! They work in tandem to support your team's efforts, much like what you see in soccer."

———

"So, we know innovation doesn't emanate from individuals; it lives in the social network," Toni said, grabbing her coffee.

"Which helps us to understand the importance of people functioning interdependently," added Jim.

"You bet. If people on your team are all functioning independently, where's your social network?" Toni said, shrugging her shoulders.

Jim nodded.

"So, Jim—what things need to change about who you are in order for your team to go where it needs to go?"

"That's a loaded question, Toni!"

They both laughed.

"OK. I'll settle for one thing."

Jim paused. "Just based on our conversation today, I would say I need to change my skill set to be more responsive to the team."

"Any examples?"

Jim pondered her question before finally answering. "Things like *active listening* instead of lecturing, *influencing* instead of controlling, and *valuing differences* instead of homogeneity—these come to mind as important changes to make if I'm going to be effective as the team's leader."

"Great answer Jim. I like that you picked up on active listening. My business partner ranks this as the number two competency—out of ten—for 'remote' team leadership based on his 2021 research.

Although active listening is not listed directly as an essential competency in our collaborative leadership platform, I like to believe we've got it covered, via the relationship building competency and its prevalence throughout our team platform—and the communicativeness competency. As I recall, relationship building is listed or overlaps five times across eleven team principles and communicativeness is listed twice.

"Active listing could be embedded in the relationship building competency," Jim offered without hesitation.

"Another great observation Jim."

"Thanks Toni."

"I can also add that nine out ten competencies listed in his research results are covered in our team platform!"

14

LET'S DANCE

Frustrated. That's how Jim felt. He knew that conflicts were a fact of life. This was especially true in teams. Toni remarked on that earlier when she'd introduced all of the essential competencies in the team's platform and mentioned conflict management as a valuable competency to apply when conflict surfaced.

Team building would take up most of Jim's morning. He gathered his team in the conference room. Each IT specialist in the field connected with them via Zoom.

"Our agenda today is to share our MBTI results," Jim began. "I think we're ready to get started."

Heads started bobbing on the screen except for one. A few people in the room played with their cell phones. Jim launched the meeting.

"Thanks for completing your MBTI assessments," Jim continued. I think we're ready to take the next step and share our results," he said confidently. "The endgame is to use this information to build our self-awareness. We also want to create a team profile."

David, his London-based IT specialist, spoke up. "I'm not comfortable with sharing my information."

A few heads around the table nodded. Andy jumped in. "Same here."

Jim was confused. "At the front end of this process, we all agreed to do this. What changed?"

Silence. Then, eventually, the two who had spoken up began to share their thoughts. Jim listened carefully to David's and Andy's concerns. The more feedback he heard from his team, the more he was convinced that he needed Toni's help to sort things out in a positive way.

He ended the meeting with a commitment to get back with them soon.

———

"What's up?" Toni asked, walking into Jim's office the following morning.

Jim paused. "I've got a problem."

"Is it a people problem or a technical problem?" she asked with a wry smile.

"As you know, Toni, we've completed the MBTI assessments for everyone on the team. However, a few of my people are pushing back on the idea of sharing their results with the other team members."

"OK. What else?"

"At the front end of this process, we all agreed to share this feedback in order to establish the team's profile and identify team strengths and weaknesses."

"That's what I remember. So, what are they saying?"

"Two people are concerned about being replaced if I'm not satisfied with the team's results."

"Just to clarify, people are thinking that you may replace them based on your preference for a particular MBTI personality type?"

Jim swallowed. "I'm guessing that's what they're saying."

"Say more."

"They're concerned about being replaced in order to establish a team profile that is a better fit for what we are being asked to do."

"Offsetting a team's weaknesses by adding people of other personality types can happen if the team is expanding. It may also happen when people leave on their own and you recruit new people. It's just an option that you or any other leader may or may not exercise."

Jim nodded.

Choosing her words carefully, Toni said, "Based on the work we did with the team when we launched this process, I did not anticipate this reaction. But I can understand and appreciate their feedback."

Jim said nothing.

———

After taking a short break to grab some coffee, Jim asked, "What are your thoughts on how to resolve this conflict?"

"Are you ready for another metaphor?" Toni asked, hoping to lighten the tone of the conversation.

"Always! So far, you're two for two, as I recall, with the metaphors."

They both smiled.

"OK, here's another one: think of conflict as a dance."

"Any dance?"

"It's all about the limited number of steps in any dance people take to complete the dance routine."

He paused to let it sink in. "OK, in my team's dance, what are the steps?" he asked with a twinkle in his eye.

"Well, there are various conflict modes—or steps—to perform in order to complete the dance in a positive way. Before we go there, however, I want to mention an important point about your team members' MBTI profiles."

"Sounds good."

"First, your team's MBTI profiles can be used to help depersonalize conflict. Although we didn't mention this to the people on your team when we launched the process, we can do that shortly."

"Can you clarify that?"

"Sure, Jim. As you're now learning, there are differences in types, including styles of perceiving and decision making. As an ISTJ type, for example, you may tend to overlook the feelings of others on the team."

"OK."

"And, as people come to understand the MBTI and those on the team of different types, they will learn how to effectively communicate and even argue in a positive, or constructive, way."

"Sounds like you're addressing the *why* question here, Toni."

"Good point, Jim. We're talking about understanding why people on teams work together effectively."

"Or not," Jim muttered.

"Mapping your team by MBTI type will help both you and other team members identify where points of conflict most likely will occur."

"How the team may be split or polarized?"

"For sure, Jim. This also deals with how each type on the team deals with change."

"That's good to hear, since change can be threatening if people don't understand it."

"Another good point, Jim."

"What next steps do you suggest to get this process completed?"

"At a minimum, we need to meet with those individuals on the team who expressed concerns and resolve these in a productive way. That way, we can get the mapping process completed and start training people on its benefits to the team. I can facilitate that discussion, if you'd like."

"I like that idea. I know this is all part of establishing base camp for the team."

Toni nodded. "In terms of team building, we're definitely in the formation stage. This requires our support to get their buy-in, or commitment, to develop their competence for using the MBTI."

———

"Is this a good time to go back to the dancing lesson you were about to give me?" Jim asked, returning from lunch.

"Sure, Jim. I wasn't looking at it as a lesson, but I can roll with that."

They both laughed.

"Obviously, we know that one requirement for teams to collaborate effectively is the ability to resolve conflict openly and constructively."

"Agree."

"This is something that gets described in your team's norms. For example, how will the team honor different decision-making styles? What rules will the team use to make decisions? Consensus, majority rule, and 'leader makes the decision after consulting with others' are a few choices here."

Jim nodded.

"Another option for you and the team to consider using when it comes to managing conflict is a tool called the Thomas Kilmann Conflict Mode Instrument®, or TKI®, as most of us call it."

"What's involved here?"

"Well, first you answer a very short list of questions. Once that's completed, the TKI produces a profile describing five conflict-handling modes one uses in the kinds of conflicts faced in our work. All five modes represent a set of useful social skills. Most of us use some of the modes more readily than the others, and we show a clear favorite over time."

"Sounds like it may be helpful for team building."

"For sure, Jim. It's proven to be extremely useful."

"So, each of these five modes represents a step in the dance you mentioned earlier?"

"Yes, Jim. The modes are basic choices you have available to manage team conflict."

"Please tell me more," Jim said, eager to understand its application.

"As with the MBTI, the idea here is to have a tool that not only recognizes how people on the team manage conflict, but also values other conflict styles."

"So, most people have a dominant style?"

"Yes. The idea is to honor that in a way that produces a positive outcome."

"Makes sense. What can you say about the team's conflict style?"

"Good question, Jim. Like the MBTI, this tool produces a team profile describing the conflict mode preferred by your team as a whole."

"Wow, that does sound helpful."

"Let me send you a booklet describing the TKI in detail. In fact, I will also send you the TKI survey to take so you get a firsthand experience. After you go through this material, we can talk some more about using it if you're interested."

"Great. Thanks, Toni."

"One last comment. One of the five conflict modes is collaboration!"

————

"You look like you had a good day," Diane said as Jim walked into the house humming a familiar tune.

"Yeah, it wasn't bad. I'm learning a new dance!"

Diane raised her eyebrow in surprise. "You're joking, right?"

"No, not really."

"What is that all about?" Diane asked, turning to face him.

"Toni hit me with a new metaphor for managing conflict on the team. She described it as a dance."

"Well, you know how I love dancing," grinned Diane. "Tell me more."

Jim thought about it for a minute. "I've got some conflict on the team that needs to be resolved. When I told Toni, she mentioned dancing as one way to think about conflict in a positive way."

Diane paused to let the concept sink in. "How soon will your dancing lessons be completed?" she asked, forcing a smile from Jim.

"Hard to tell. You know I can be pretty clumsy."

They both laughed.

15

PLAY ON!

"Jim, what would be most helpful to focus on right now?" Toni asked as the two walked out of Brett's office. They'd been bringing Brett up-to-date on the coaching process and Jim's progress with it.

Hesitating slightly, Jim said, "I'm not sure."

Toni sensed an opportunity. "What one thing do you need to focus on in order to take your team to the next level?"

"Good question, Toni. As you know, I had members of the team complete their competency self-assessments. Then we restated each person's developmental goal. Everyone seemed to be onboard, but a few of the people have been reluctant to get started."

Toni was curious. "What are they saying?

"I'm not sure if they've bought in to the need to collaborate as a team."

"Everyone, or just the members that have been dragging their feet?"

"I'm not sure, to be honest. For the sake of argument, let's just say everyone."

"There may be one thing I can suggest to clarify the importance of applying collaboration in the team's daily work."

"Go ahead."

"Your coaching challenge is to get people to understand that high performance is needed for the task at hand—and it can only be achieved when everyone functions in a way that recognizes the interdependent nature of team members' relationships with each other and various stakeholders."

"So, anything short of that understanding would mean that people are not practicing team collaboration?"

"Exactly. Keep in mind, however, that high performance may not be needed for all tasks. As the team's leader, this is a situation you need to address when necessary."

"I'm hearing you say collaboration may not be the team's default for all tasks. Correct?"

"Spot-on, Jim. Because the need to collaborate is task specific, at times your team may function in a way that does not require collaboration. It can be a fine line to manage, but if interdependence is not needed to complete the task, then there's no need to collaborate. Make sense?"

"Got it."

———

"What else fed into this reluctance you discovered in your team?" Toni asked, arriving at Jim's office.

"I'm not sure this is related. Two of my team members seem to struggle with understanding the principles I introduced earlier."

"What's your gut telling you?"

"That's a tough question for someone who prefers using his senses to gather information," Jim said with a wry smile.

They both laughed.

"It could be resistance to change. Or it could be a training issue."

"Or both," Toni offered.

Jim thought about it for a moment. "Since we've only had a limited amount of time to understand the principles, I'm going to go with lack of training."

"OK, that sounds like a fair conclusion. May I make a recommendation?"

Jim nodded. "Of course."

"One option is to schedule a training program another business partner and I developed and use with clients," Toni said. "It's called, 'The Collaboration Game,' and it's a good way to expedite the development of the principles and the competencies embedded in the platform. In fact, let me test it on your two people who are struggling to understand the principles. I'll set that up for tomorrow."

"Sounds good on both fronts. Send me the details on the training program, and I will run it by Brett."

———

The following morning, Toni set up the training program in the conference room. Her plan was to use this opportunity to resolve a real conflict between the product development and the information technology departments. The conflict was centered on the need to collaborate on a project. The resulting confusion and tension triggered a slowdown. Deadlines loomed and pressure to complete the project had increased.

Four people entered the conference room. Table teams representing each of the two departments were established. Jim's two reluctant collaborators represented the information technology team. Toni led both teams through a brief orientation, telling them their task was to function with a collaborative mind-set, using the principles, in the training simulation she was about to present.

Over the course of the next hour, each team played a game answering a series of six cards. Each card described a specific challenge. Based on the way in which the team decided to resolve each challenge, they were awarded points. Embedded in each challenge was the option to select a solution that demonstrated a collaborative mind-set. Teams who were able to identify and select options that embraced the application of the principles were deemed most effective, awarded more points, and crowned the winner.

Toni then ran both teams through a debriefing. The purpose was to share their experiences, answer questions, and solidify the knowledge they'd gained.

She was convinced Jim's two people were now onboard with the need to collaborate with product development on the project.

"How did things go?" Jim asked Toni once she'd wrapped up the training session.

"I was happy with the experience. Your two people seemed to get it. They told me they were good to go now that they fully understood how the principles are applied."

"I will be sure to pass that along to Brett. That should help influence his decision to continue to support your training proposal."

After a short break, Toni and Jim continued their conversation about building his team's understanding of the principles. "Along with the training program," Toni said, "can you think of ways to build repetition into your coaching routine using the principles?"

"Let me give that some thought."

"This may be your key coaching challenge in the beginning. I know you've got the principles listed in your team's charter. That's good. However, your challenge is to embed these into your team's actions; it's not enough for them to simply understand, agree with, or appreciate them."

"Sounds like we're talking about developing team habits."

"Exactly. Perhaps you can do some brainstorming and come up with a list of applications. We can review your list the next time we meet. How's that sound?"

Jim nodded.

Toni believed that developing the team's mind-set would challenge Jim. It would require her coaching help in the short term and Jim's coaching in the long term. It was obviously a critical step. Functioning with a collaborative mind-set using the principles would not only would help shape, or frame, the team's application of essential competencies, but would also serve to motivate the team members' interest and desire to acquire the needed competence, or skill set, to produce win-win solutions. Through the process of developing competencies aligned with each principle, people on the team would start to acquire a deeper understanding and appreciation of what it means to function with a collaborative mind-set. She liked to describe this process as a never-ending cycle, with mind-set affirming skill set—and skill set affirming mind-set.

The next afternoon found Jim juggling his schedule yet again. Rescuing people on his team was becoming time consuming. Chasing after them in regard to various matters was something he was not accustomed to doing.

He managed to get Kate, one of his IT specialists, squared away on her assignment just as he learned that Andy had an issue needing his attention. *One down and one to go*, he thought as he made his way back to his office.

"What's going on?" Jim asked, catching Andy in the hallway.

"Must be the weather. Our gray days make people behave in ways that don't make sense." He pulled out his notebook, flipping pages to find what he wanted to share with Jim.

"I think the weather is more predictable than people," Jim said, sitting down in his office.

Andy looked up. Jim's words had caught him by surprise. It was the first time Andy had heard this from him.

"What've you got?" Jim asked, knowing the clock was ticking.

Later that afternoon Jim bumped into Toni, who was on the property to meet with a potential coaching client.

"Jim, I've got an hour before I have to meet with another client," Toni said. "You look like you've had a busy day. Is there anything you want to cover before I take off?"

Jim was quiet. Toni asked, "How are you dealing with stress? I know you've got a lot on your plate."

"I'm just feeling a little stressed out, I guess."

Toni was curious. "I'm not surprised to hear that, Jim. On a scale of one to ten, where is your stress level right now?"

Jim paused before answering. "Perhaps seven or eight, I'm guessing."

"That's not good," Toni said, bluntly. "When was the last time your stress was significantly lower?"

Again, Jim said nothing.

"Perhaps we can talk about your feelings, Jim. What are they saying?"

Toni knew that highly effective leaders are conscious of their feelings. She also knew this would need to become a significant part of Jim's growth strategy if he was going to succeed in his career.

Pondering, Jim did not answer Toni's question.

Sensing an opening, Toni said, "Jim, I know that, as an ISTJ type, you may find it challenging to deal with feelings. But it's important not to suppress your feelings."

"I feel like I'm starting to lose control, and I'm getting frustrated," he finally said.

"What does that feel like?"

"Besides stressing me out, it's like being thrown around by a tornado. Sort of a helpless feeling, if you know what I mean."

"Helpless; that sounds extreme. Say a little more, Jim."

Hesitating before answering, Jim finally said, "I feel like I'm in a free fall. Like I'm functioning in a limited way. It's almost paralyzing."

"What would you like to feel instead?"

"I would like to feel like I've got more control over my work and life, for example," Jim explained.

Toni continued to probe. "And how would that feel?"

"Great!" he declared. "Functioning properly in my job. Being able to have time with my family. That would feel great."

"Jim, that's good feedback for me as your coach. Unfortunately, I've got to head to my next appointment. Let's plan to pick this up tomorrow—is that OK with you?"

"Sounds OK," Jim said, relieved for the moment.

"Thanks, Jim. So, to briefly summarize, you feel a loss of control in your new job. This has limited how you function. Have I got that right? And let's not forget about family!"

Jim nodded.

———

On her way to meet up with her next client, Toni continued to think about Jim's feedback. She had not been surprised to hear him say he was experiencing added stress in his job and family life. It was something she'd anticipated. Asking Jim about his stress level was her way of being proactive in her coaching. While this felt like a minor regression in his level of commitment to become a collaborative leader, she was optimistic her coaching would win the day and get Jim through this bump in the road. Most people, including Toni herself, experience some level of regression in their commitment level after taking on a new task such as learning to play an instrument or even making a purchase. Often described as "buyer's remorse," it was a feeling that required added support from her and others.

16

CULTURE TRUMPS STRATEGY

S lammed. That's how Jim felt as he reviewed his schedule and reflected on the stress and uncertainty he'd felt in his new position these past few weeks. The everyday reality of juggling and managing many tasks was something he was not used to, but he would need to learn how to do it if he wanted to be successful.

Jim knew his entire day would be spent reading the survey reports—all twenty-seven of them—generated by the product development, sales, and IT departments. The surveys consisted of a series of questions that would provide him with feedback on the IT department's performance over the past two to three months. Although he knew the feedback might not address collaboration specifically, he thought it might offer some insights into relationships and general performance concerns. As he slowly made his way through the information, he took notes and tried to maintain his focus. Halfway through the process, he took a break and went for a short walk. His emotions were steady, yet he knew he could explode at any time. It was apparent the survey results produced two major themes. The first one dealt with a lack of trust inside the team at each sales office. The second theme suggested a lack of team leadership in the IT department—a theme that struck a personal chord.

Toni called just as he'd begun to draft a report to share with her and Brett. "How's the review coming?"

"I'm processing the feedback as we speak," Jim admitted. He pushed back in his chair, taking a deep breath before continuing. "So far, I've got them organized by function." Leaning over, he quickly shuffled each pile to keep them separated.

"What's the verdict?"

Jim eased into a standing position before speaking. Fighting to stifle a quiver in his voice, he shared his feedback with Toni.

"How are you feeling?"

"I felt a little betrayed, if that makes sense."

"Were you surprised by the feedback?"

Jim pondered the question before responding. "Not really. But I probably let it affect me in a negative way."

"You just got initiated! You can't grow unless you're willing to accept feedback for what it is and not take it personally."

Toni waited for Jim to speak.

Nothing.

"So," continued Toni, "judging by what you've shared with me, not only are your IT specialists here in Portland failing to function as a team, but in addition, your IT specialists in the field are failing to partner with their salespeople."

"That's it in a nutshell," Jim blurted out.

"When I was in the military, we had a similar challenge. We had to develop multiple teams across the organization to support each team's ability to add value and achieve goals. We described it as developing a network of teams."

As he listened to Toni address the issue in a matter-of-fact, yet supportive way, Jim began to calm down.

"I'm guessing the underlying issue for your teams may be lack of trust," Toni continued. "The challenge is to develop trust inside and across your teams so people feel free to connect and function interdependently."

Relieved for the moment, Jim said, "Makes sense."

Toni's description reminded Jim of the way he'd seen soccer players function interdependently. Because trust had been developed, players were able to connect as needed to move the ball on the field. Most important, he'd observed, were players passing the ball to an open space on the field, expecting or trusting teammates to get to the ball before an opponent.

"Once you finalize the feedback from the surveys," Toni explained, "we'll be able to complete a game plan to tackle your next steps. We'll also work on your development plan."

Toni was not overly concerned about Jim's reaction to the survey feedback. She knew he may get disillusioned from time to time about his team's development—and he may even experience a regression in his commitment level. She was confident Jim would be able to get through this with her help.

Jim read over his report on the surveys before sending it to Toni and Brett. He'd suggested to Toni to include Brett in this process, and she'd agreed. They were planning to meet the following day.

————

"So, it looks like we have quite a bit of work to do," Brett said as the three gathered in his office.

"Yeah," Jim admitted. "The survey results produced a couple of overlapping themes we need to address. The first one deals with a lack of trust inside the team at each office. The second theme deals with a lack of team leadership at the department level."

"Toni, what's your take on these results?" Brett asked.

"On the one hand, I'm not surprised to see trust surface as an issue. That issue has come up with many of the teams and organizations I've dealt with. It's especially common among new teams."

"Jim, what else?" Brett asked.

Jim paused before answering. "The feedback about the department's leadership is not very positive."

Toni jumped in. "Let me clarify what Jim is referring to. The feedback refers to the former manager of the IT services department, not to Jim. I guess that's the good news. The bad news is that Jim needs to be responsive to their needs—and that needs to happen sooner, not later!"

"I agree," Brett said. "I was just getting ready to tackle this matter before Jim came onboard."

Smiling, Toni nodded.

"Sounds like we need to set up base camp for my IT team," Jim said.

"Yes. That's the first step," Toni said. "After that, we can look at what needs to happen with team development at each of the four sales offices. Because these are cross-functional teams, the challenge will be more complex."

"No doubt," said Brett. "I will need to connect with the VP of sales to get his understanding and support before we implement any changes at each sales office. Since we have a strong commitment to develop teams and a culture of collaboration throughout the company, that should not be a major concern."

"That's a huge positive when it comes to collaboration," Toni said. "Research shows, without a supportive culture, collaboration eludes organizations."

———

"Good meeting," Jim said, walking back to his office with Toni.

"Yes, I thought so. It's critical to have a culture that supports the development of team collaboration. For example, I've seen organizations rely solely on technology to drive their collaboration development efforts, and it has not worked. Technology is important, but it's only an enabler. Investing in technology without investing in people and their interpersonal skills—including team leadership and their management skills—is not productive."

"Speaking personally, that's good to hear. I can't imagine trying to succeed in my new job without training and support. That includes coaching."

Toni was grateful for the opportunity to work with Jim, Brett, and other stakeholders. Her coaching relationship with Jim was working well. As his coach, she was focusing mostly on developmental coaching rather than performance coaching. The former application addressed the development of Jim's competencies and capacity in his new role, while the latter would involve coaching to help him become a more effective contributor to the organization's goals. Coaching Jim's team, however, required another shift in style; in that capacity, she often functioned "in the moment" using a hybrid style that combined consulting and coaching. She recalled that, during her training as a team coach, her trainer—a well-known global authority on team coaching—told her that, in team coaching, people on the team wanted the coach to bring everything to the table to help the team succeed. Everything meant everything—knowledge, experience, ideas, suggestions, and more. At the time, Toni had been a little surprised to hear his feedback, since it was different from the way in which she'd been initially trained as a coach. That training promoted a coaching style, described as "leading from behind," using questions to generate a coaching discussion in order to support a client's individual development.

Sitting quietly in Jim's office, Toni wondered if this would be a good time to deal with Jim's stress. "Jim, is this a good time to pick up our conversation from yesterday?"

"As good a time as any, I guess. Go ahead."

"OK, Jim. Let me ask you, what one thing would make the biggest difference in your stress level?"

Jim swallowed and said nothing.

Toni pushed on. "You mentioned feeling a loss of control in your job. What's one change you can make to help relieve your stress?"

Jim nodded. "Last night I was thinking about this. Perhaps I need to find a way to compartmentalize my work so that I don't feel so overwhelmed. Does that make sense?"

"Absolutely. That would help minimize or eliminate any nonessential responsibilities. It would also give you more time to plan, and it would make it easier for you to put some order into your routine."

"Can you help with that?"

"For sure. It's an ability you can develop with a little coaching. Let's jump on that tomorrow."

"Anything else you can suggest to help deal with my stress?" Jim asked before ending his coaching session with Toni.

"You bet. Let's try this, Jim." Toni quickly began to jot down some notes. "Here are a few basic options, based on your MBTI profile, you can think about; they may well help to relieve your stress. We can kick these around once you've decided what may work for you."

Jim quickly scanned the notes Toni had written for him.

1. Find a way to build some alone time into your daily routine.
2. Exercise daily.
3. Talk things over with a good friend who will listen without judging.

Jim nodded.

"I can help you with the third option, but I would encourage you to find someone else to talk to as well. Perhaps Dan?"

———

Jim's staying at work a little later tonight, thought Diane with concern. Since taking on his new job, Jim had not shared a lot about his feelings with her, but she'd suspected something was really bothering him. Finally, last night he confided he was finding his work and his new position very stressful. She hoped that Jim's coach could help him effectively deal with this.

"How was your day?" Diane asked, as Jim came through the door.

17

TRANSCEND TECHNIQUE

An emphasis on relationship building creates a very demanding position for most people and organizations, Toni believed as she prepared to meet with Jim. Technology continues to make it easier for all of us to avoid the interpersonal, face-to-face communication that is so important to establishing and maintaining both personal and professional relationships. Yet we all know people—including leaders—whose success is totally dependent upon their ability to transcend technology or technique and deal with people on a relationship basis to achieve results.

"What's on your mind?" Toni asked, approaching Jim in his office.

"Toni, I understand that building self-awareness takes time and commitment. Are there any shortcuts I can use with my team to help build the team's self-awareness?"

"What else?"

"I guess I'm looking for any tools or techniques that would help to move the team's development along at a faster pace."

Smiling, Toni nodded. "What's the real challenge here for developing your team?"

Again, Jim paused. "How to motivate the team, I'm thinking."

Toni knew that motivation was a word had come to mean all things to all people. That is, most people think of motivation the way they think of quality; they can't define it, but they know it when they see it. She liked to describe it as an energy that, once seen or experienced, is the ultimate intangible to help people and teams achieve results.

"Could it be a commitment issue?" Toni asked.

Good point, Jim thought. "Toni, you have a knack for quickly getting to the 'root-cause' of the problem with your coaching questions."

Toni smiled. "Jim, many years ago I had the opportunity to hear an expert talk about leadership. He said that leadership is first about relationships and relationship building; it's not just a matter of acquired expertise or technique. He even said that, if he had to give something up, it would not be relationship building!"

"OK, so I need to find ways to leverage my relationship with the team to help gain their commitment to perform."

"Yes. Can I also suggest you find out how people on your team are building relationships with each other?"

"For sure," Jim said, relieved for the moment.

Toni pushed forward. "You and your team also need to think about the importance of relationship building on several levels. This is what makes it so important and challenging to your team's success."

"Tell me more."

"Not only is relationship building important inside your IT team, but it's also important for each individual IT member at their respective sales office to establish relationships with their key sales stakeholders. That may seem obvious, but it's very important to ensuring collaboration."

"Agree."

Toni continued. "And from there, it's a case of each team establishing relationships with key stakeholders or customers their offices serve."

"Wow! I'd never thought about it that way."

Toni smiled again. "That's why I like to describe collaboration as a team sport. Your organization's success is highly dependent on adding value as a network of teams."

Toni was delighted to see Jim starting to really understand why relationship building was important to his success as a first-time leader.

This would go a long way toward helping him develop his emotional intelligence as well.

———

"Any concerns or challenges so far pertaining to leading your team?" Toni asked Jim before grabbing some coffee.

"That's a timely question," Jim said, collecting his thoughts. "I'm not sure, but it might be related to selling."

"Sounds interesting. Tell me more."

"I don't think I sell ideas very well. For example, I'm trying to motivate my people to understand and proactively apply our operating platform, but it seems like there is a lot of selling going on and not too much buying at the moment."

"What have you tried so far?"

"I've reviewed the platform with everyone and directed them to go back and review the material you provided. I set up goals to get them started on developing their strengths in regard to targeted competencies. And, I recently got approval on the training course you suggested earlier, so that should help, too—I hope."

"So, it sounds like you've been proactive with your people, Jim, and that's good. Can I make a suggestion?" Jim nodded.

"Here's an idea with some science behind it. In selling ideas or trying to influence people, it helps to address what is called 'the why question.' For example, why is the company developing a collaborative culture? Why is team collaboration so important to the company? Why does the company use coaching as a tool to support people and team development? I could go on, but I think you get my drift."

"To support the company's business objectives," Jim stated.

"Absolutely. 'Business growth through innovation' is what we heard Brett say. And that requires collaboration."

"Go on."

"How well do your people understand the why question, Jim? At the end of the day, for example, are current circumstances or business difficulties—real or anticipated—understood well enough by your people to provide motivation for change?"

Jim paused before responding, "I can't sit here and answer that question with a yes."

"OK. This is one option you might want to use to help you inspire your people and gain their commitment."

"I see what you're saying."

"Your coaching challenge includes getting people to understand why collaboration is needed to support the company's goals and objectives. Again, that includes understanding why high performance is needed for the task at hand—and it can be achieved only when everyone functions in a way that recognizes the interdependent nature of the team's relationship with each other and all stakeholders."

18

HIT PLAY ▶

"How would you like to use the balance of our time today?" Toni asked, ready to head out for lunch.

"Not sure." Just then they were greeted by Brett.

"Hey, guys," Brett said, "I just came by to ask when you were scheduling Toni's training program. I would like to attend, if that's OK."

"It's scheduled for two weeks from today," Jim said. "I've got all members of my team coming in for the workshop, so that will give us ten participants including you."

"Great," Brett said. "I'm looking forward to learning how it's used to develop a collaborative mind-set and skill set."

"Me too," Jim said, turning to Toni.

Everyone smiled.

"Looks like your heading out for lunch," Brett said, walking to the door. "Can I buy?"

———

After sitting down for lunch, Toni thought it would be a good time to offer Jim and Brett some added background on her training program, since they both seemed keen to learn more.

"Since I've got a captive audience," Toni said, "let me take this opportunity to fill you in about our upcoming training program—if that works for you?"

"Great," Jim said.

"Love to hear more," Brett agreed. "Since I approved the proposal, it would be nice to learn more about what I signed off on," he said, grinning.

Everyone smiled.

"OK, then," Toni said. "As you both know, The Collaboration Game was developed by my business partner and me to help people on teams develop a collaborative mind-set and skill set to effectively collaborate."

"Can you tell us about your business partner?" Brett asked.

"Sure. He's an expert in designing board game simulations," Toni said. "As I recall, he has over twenty-five years of experience in board game simulation design, development, and delivery, and he's worked for several leading training companies."

"What's a board game simulation?" Brett asked.

"Good question, Brett," Toni replied. "It's an experiential training program presented via a board game, like Monopoly® or Parcheesi®, where players simulate a team working to resolve various business projects and challenges using a series of vignettes or mini cases. Usually, three to five people play as a team. The Collaboration Game uses soccer as a theme—again, because soccer represents an environment where people have to collaborate effectively to succeed. The team that makes collaborative choices ends up with the best score in the game."

"So, you took your business partner's expertise and combined it with your content knowledge to come up with the game?" Brett asked.

"Exactly," Toni said.

"Why a board game?" Jim asked.

"Well, as you know, our operating platform describes desired behaviors for team collaboration—but presenting the content as 'the desired state' will fall flat with participants in the absence of a chance to experience its associated behaviors, both good and bad. This makes for an excellent opportunity for a board game."

"Can you tell us more about why board game simulations work so well?" Jim asked.

Toni nodded. "By inviting people to play a simulation like ours, we provide an opportunity for them to discuss the distinctions and tradeoffs of their decisions. In addition, the game helps them connect the dots between desired behaviors and real business results that illustrate why an organization places so much emphasis on top performance—in this case, top performance in terms of team collaboration."

"Hands-on practice always worked for me," Jim said. "You answered my question. Thanks, Toni."

"It's a great question, Jim. The distinction between board game simulations and other training formats is a critical one to understand," Toni explained.

"Please say more," Brett said.

"By playing a board game simulation like ours, people actually experience the *how* and *why* of the desired team behavior the exercise is designed to convey."

Heads nodded.

Toni continued. "The retention and application of the behaviors experienced in the simulation will greatly improve the participants' return on their investment in the training workshop."

"I like hearing that," Brett said.

"Just imagine the benefits from this kind of training experience!" Toni said.

"Thanks for sharing," Jim said. "I can't wait to participate in the program. My team should really benefit from this experience as well."

"It will also be fun," Toni said, smiling. "The workshop is fast paced, content rich, and highly interactive."

————

"If I were watching your team in six months, what team dynamics would I see?" Toni asked Jim as they returned to the office after lunch.

"Wow! That's a question I didn't see coming."

"No worries, Jim. I'm not looking for you to answer it today."

They both laughed.

"I'll put that question on hold until you have an answer for me," Toni said.

"I get your point, Toni. I have my work cut out for me in terms of knowing what to expect in the future."

"My vision for you and your team, including each sales office team, calls for succeeding at 'game of teams' in six months," Toni said emphatically.

Jim paused to let her declaration sink in. "That's my hope and plan too. We should be well on our way, applying a collaborative mind-set and skill set to harness the power of connections across all of our networks and creating added value to support all of our stakeholders."

"At which time I can call you a collaborative leader!"

Jim smiled.

———

"Hey, Dan, guess what I'm going to be doing in a few weeks?" Jim said, sitting down to meet with his friend after work.

"Planning a vacation, I'm guessing."

"Not even close. I'm planning to play soccer for the first time!"

Curious, Dan asked, "What's that all about?"

"Glad you asked. We've scheduled a team development training program to teach people how to effectively collaborate. Toni helped develop the program. It uses the game of soccer to teach people how to develop a collaborative mind-set for applying a collaborative skill set. "

Smiling, Dan said, "I told you earlier that Toni's got your team's development all figured out!"

"You know, I think you're right," Jim said, grinning back at Dan.

PART 5

Conclusion

19

GAME ON

"How's the team's development coming along?" Toni asked Jim over the phone. "Have you come up with a plan to develop an innovative solution for your customer in London?"

"As you know, we're planning to start a project launch next week, and we'll extend it over the following four weeks. All meetings will be virtual. After that, we've got the offsite meeting planned to bring everyone together face-to-face. That should help us move quickly through the forming stage."

"As we've discussed in the past, you need to be proactive in the forming stage in order to avoid moving into the storming stage and instead get to the norming stage," Toni cautioned.

"Toni, I think we've got the team well positioned to tackle this challenge. With your coaching support, we should be in good shape."

Toni knew Jim had made the right call to get her involved early in this project's launch. Since team coaching was a relationship, not an event, it was important to have some added face time with Jim's group.

———

The following Wednesday came quickly. Toni was planning to meet with Jim and his immediate team, which consisted of the four local IT specialists along with all four field IT specialists. The in-house people would be linking up with field IT specialists over Zoom.

Even though the London IT specialist was the only one directly involved with this project, Jim made it clear earlier he wanted everyone involved on each project's launch. This, he believed, would help to develop the team—and perhaps even expedite a project's status. The plan today was for Jim to start working with his own team; then they would expand the group of people involved in the project to include the sales members of the cross-functional team in London.

After his team had gathered together, Jim kicked things off by setting expectations for the meeting. He then reintroduced Toni, who had met everyone at the team's training program two months earlier.

Toni jumped in. "Good morning. It's great to be here and work with Jim and the team on this project."

All heads nodded across the room and on the screen.

"I thought it would make sense to provide a quick overview of my role as Jim's coach on this project. After that, Jim will walk through several protocols that have been established to help get this project launch rolling. Time permitting, he can also review the team's future development plans."

"Sounds like a good plan," Jim said. "I should also mention that Toni is scheduled to join us at each meeting for the next month."

Jim knew scheduling Toni to be a part of the team's first project launch was his way of ensuring her past efforts to develop and support him and the team would not be lost due to his inexperience. Without her, he knew the likelihood of his failing was high. She was his insurance card. With her as his coach, he knew defeat was highly unlikely.

"Thanks, Jim," Toni said. "So, my primary role on this project is to support Jim's development. It's my hope that, by doing so, you'll be better equipped to meet future stakeholder expectations. Since Jim's team coaching is carried out in the moment, my value to Jim and the team comes whenever an issue crops up that interferes with the team's ability to execute the plan. That's pretty much how I add value."

Again, heads nodded.

As Jim's coach, I should also say I'm not here to replace Jim as your leader coach. In the beginning of this engagement, you can expect to see more of me, since Jim is still in the process of developing his own skills as a leader coach. It's a process that takes time — and most likely, formal training."

"Any questions," Jim asked, making eye contact with everyone in the room and on the screen.

Silence.

"OK, let's look at some key protocols we've got in place to support the team's efforts to collaborate," Jim said. "Let's start with the principles. As we all know, these are embedded in the team's charter to describe how we work together as a team. The plan is to eventually extend these to others in our network, since we are trying to build a network of teams. We just signed up our product development group on these, so that's our first internal partner outside of sales."

"Perfect, Toni said. "I look forward to the team getting an external partner, such as a supplier, to come onboard as well."

"Me too," Jim said.

"As you recall from playing the Collaboration Game, the best way to learn and develop the principles is to find ways to embed them into your team's thinking and actions," Toni said.

"Building repetition is a key here," Jim said, recalling Toni's words from an earlier conversation.

"Let's move on to talk about the team's MBTI profile," Jim said, glancing at the screen. "As you all know, we've established this to build self-awareness. After mapping each person's type profile, we now have a way to deal with team dynamics in a productive way. For example, the team's profile takes into account norms likely to emerge and whether they fit our team approach to the work we're doing."

"Will you or Toni be providing more coaching pertaining to the team's profile?" Jana, the Los Angeles IT specialist, asked.

"I guarantee it will come up frequently," Toni said, "especially when we're dealing with conflict resolution and fostering innovation."

"Obviously, those are two very important issues for us," Jim said.

"Speaking of conflict resolution," Jim added, we also have the TKI established as a protocol, or tool, to help produce positive outcomes. Again, it's a case of using this tool to honor individuals' differences for building and maintaining productive relationships inside the team."

"That will also help everybody deal effectively with the team's need for psychological safety," Toni added.

"Any questions," Jim asked, looking over at Toni.

————

After taking a short break to address a technical matter, Jim and Toni resumed their conference call with the team.

"Toni, what's next on the agenda to cover today?"

"A couple of things, Jim. Now that the team has some comfort with the principles, it's important to create new processes that are not leader dependent. Because we're asking the team to respond to changing conditions on their own, for example, your team needs to establish processes that allow them to make decisions, take risks, adapt, and the like—processes that provide the freedom to perform the work and produce win-win outcomes."

"Makes sense," Jim said. "Any examples?"

"One idea is to develop criteria to assess innovative ideas and suggestions. That way, the team can continue its innovation efforts without having to run everything past you, for example. Like soccer, the innovation game is played in a continuous way. And, again, we all agree that speed is critical here."

Pondering, Jim said, "This really brings home our earlier conversation about delegating based on trust."

Toni smiled, glancing at the team members in the room and on the screen.

"What else? Jim asked

"My other comment deals with future relationships you all establish with each cross-functional team. Bottom line: keep in mind your relationships with those teams need to be as strong as they are inside this immediate team. That can be a challenging task, to say the least—but, with the team principles in place, the team has a foundation on which to build and get this accomplished."

"One last item to mention today." Jim said. "The team's charter is in place, but it needs to be reviewed. That will take up most of our time during next week's call."

"This will always be an ongoing task for the team," Toni added.

"We will make it a priority to ensure our team's norms are always working to support collaboration," Jim added.

"Not to change the subject, but you mentioned future team development earlier," Carlos, the IT specialist from Sao Palo, said. "Can you say more?"

"You bet," Toni said. "That takes us back to the 360 survey process that's been mentioned in the past. We're soon coming up on the time to have you all complete a 360 survey to provide feedback on the essential competencies described in both your operating platform and EQ model. Since they deal with several competencies that overlap, we're able to provide a customized 360 survey to capture feedback for both applications."

"That feedback will help me identify future development opportunities for each of you," Jim said.

"When do you expect that to roll out?" asked Sei Young, the Singapore-based IT specialist.

"Good question," Toni said. "I'm thinking we'll roll it out in about sixty-ninety days. We want you all to have adequate time to get established as a team before we send out the 360 surveys."

"I know everybody's development is important and we're eager to get started, but I also want quality feedback," Jim added.

Toni was ready for the team to move forward on its journey. As Jim's coach, she anticipated that summiting its own 'Denali' was not likely to occur without missteps along the way. However, she was confident in Jim's leadership. He'd progressed quickly from being reluctant to being capable. And the team was not at all disillusioned about what the future might bring. With Jim's coaching support, they would collaborate to innovate and produce a win-win outcome for their customer in London.

———

"Any concerns?' Toni asked Jim once they'd wrapped up the meeting and were alone in the conference room.

"Just a little nervous, to be totally honest."

"That's to be expected. I always have a few butterflies when I'm involved in a project's launch. And I've been doing this for a while now."

"I'm keeping my fingers crossed that this project will go as planned and be anticlimactic, if you know what I mean, Toni."

Toni nodded. "I know what you're referring to here. There's always a chance that your faith in people to perform the work will be tested, as they say. But I'm not too concerned about that happening."

Jim smiled.

"However, you're more likely to get frustrated and question your ability to use everything you've learned to affect your team's performance if they fail to perform. Should that happen, I would describe it as losing the battle, but not the war."

Jim nodded. "Move on quickly if that happens, I guess!"

"Yes, but some find that easier said than done. If the team's failure becomes personal, it may be more challenging for you to move on quickly. Just saying."

Jim pondered Toni's feedback. "Sounds like we're back to self-awareness and managing emotions and feelings."

"Exactly."

20

INFLUENCE ME, PLEASE

"When I first met with Brett, he asked me who my favorite leader was," Jim said, sitting down to meet Toni for his scheduled coaching session. "I told him I wasn't sure if I could answer that question."

"Can you answer it now?"

Jim paused. "Still not sure."

Toni nodded. "That's fine. As you learn more about collaborative leadership, that may open possibilities to consider. I'm guessing Brett was asking you the question in an open-ended way, meaning that you could identify any leader from industry, government, sports, and the like."

"That makes sense. He said his favorite was Nelson Mandela."

Toni smiled. "I can understand why he picked him. His ability to influence others in order to achieve his goal was remarkable. To me, that is the key to effective leadership."

"The ability to influence people?"

"Absolutely! I learned early in my career that leadership is an influence process. It can be used for any reason, goal related or not. You may be trying to influence your wife, for example, to take a trip. If she says yes, then your influence, or leadership, was successful. And if her decision to take the trip leaves her with a positive attitude, then we could say your leadership was also effective."

Jim laughed. "I never thought about it that way!"

"It's a critical distinction to make when you're learning how to lead others. As a new leader, the tendency will be to influence people using positional power instead of personal power. Ideally, you want to learn how to use both to lead others. It's also important to keep in mind, you never want to give up your positional power. As boss, you never stop being a boss—that's how I like to describe it."

Again, Jim nodded. *Some more dots to connect*, he thought.

"This is especially true when it comes to collaboration," Toni pointed out.

Jim smiled. "That gets us back to Mandela and how he serves as an excellent role model."

"Exactly. Collaborative leaders like Mandela use personal power more often than, say, positional power to influence others, effectively delegating to achieve success and effectiveness."

"This also gets us back to understanding the value of relationship building as a key competency in our operating platform. Now I can appreciate why you said that earlier."

"Spot-on, Jim. Personal power comes from building and maintaining relationships."

Unfortunately, Toni thought, today most of us lament our apparent lack of collaborative leader role models at the top of many of our organizations. However, the need to effectively collaborate in order to achieve success in today's world was only increasing. She believed that more and more people, therefore, were bound to realize the critical value and competitive edge collaborative leaders bring to organizations. New leaders like Jim, Toni thought, would someday have a ready answer to Brett's question. She knew her old boss believed this as well. He was truly a collaborative leader who married his passion for leadership with his passion for soccer, introducing her to a new innovative way to collaborate. There was no doubt, Toni reflected, that she would find it very easy to tell Brett who her favorite leader was.

———

After grabbing some coffee during a short break, Toni said, "Getting back to the ways in which leaders influence others to achieve results, I thought it'd be a good idea to recap the value of our team principles when it comes to influencing peoples' efforts to effectively collaborate."

Jim nodded. "Having them embedded in our team charter is critical to operating with team norms that support collaboration."

"You should be able to see this play out soon in real time as your team learns how to find ways to collaborate to innovate for the project in London."

"Agree. People finally embraced these once they completed the training program."

"So, they were able to connect the dots."

They both smiled.

Toni pulled out her laptop and scrolled to the page listing the operating principles:

TEAM PRINCIPLES

- Focus On Team, Not Position
- Understand That Everyone Can Play
- Embrace Diversity
- Rely On Each Other
- Promote Individual & Team Values
- Seek Out Skillful, Adaptable Players
- Charge The Team To Perform the Work
- Empower Players To Win
- Coach Teams To Respond To Changing Conditions On Their Own
- Develop Partners On The Field
- Achieve Cross-Cultural Agility

"Understanding how these principles work together to influence the team's behavior is the key to practicing genuine team collaboration," Toni said.

"I know these are all in play all the time."

"Glad you remembered, Jim."

"It took a while for my people to understand why these principles are not listed in any particular order."

"That's understandable, Jim. Any time you list things, people tend to either number or rank the items."

"In this case, we know they're equal—and, when combined, are used to generate the team's synergy."

"Good point, Jim. Let's not forget, when combined, they also describe a collaborative mind-set."

Smiling, Jim nodded.

Epilogue: Do the Math

"This has been one challenging journey so far," Jim said, motioning for Toni and Brett to grab a seat in his office.

"The good news is that you've done well in managing your transition," Brett said.

"Thanks. I have to give the credit to you and Toni," Jim said.

"Don't be so modest," Toni said. "It took your inner strength to deal effectively with all of the challenges over the past six months. This includes increasing your self-awareness to help you get where you are today."

"You really demonstrated the endurance of a runner in a marathon!" Brett commented.

Toni nodded.

"This requires a certain degree of willpower, self-discipline, and perseverance, to say the least," Brett added.

"Without your coaching, Toni, and Brett's leadership, I would not be where I am today," Jim said. "And my team would not be as far along in its development."

"The team's ability to effectively collaborate has been noticed in the field by our customers and various stakeholders," Brett said.

"So, there you have it, Jim," Toni said.

"Toni, I also have to say that, since your operating platform has been launched by others in the company, we are seeing real progress in developing collaborative leaders and teams," Brett said.

"Thanks, Brett. That's great feedback."

Everyone smiled.

"Any other takeaways to share at this point, Toni?" Jim asked.

Toni paused to answer the question. There was so much going on that she really wanted to be selective in answering Jim's question. Walking over to the whiteboard, she wrote:

Globalization Without Collaboration Is Like Collaboration Without Trust

"Does that make sense?" Toni asked with a wry grin.

Brett responded immediately. "Are you saying that globalization is dead without collaboration—and that collaboration is dead without trust?"

"Yes," Toni said. "Globalization cannot survive without collaboration—and collaboration cannot exist without trust."

Everyone paused to let Toni's words sink in.

Sensing an opportunity to push on, Toni said, "The idea that we can have a globalized world without collaborating to make it work is ludicrous when you think about it."

"And trust is the key," Jim said.

"Spot-on, Jim," Toni said. "Spot-on."

Appendix

In this appendix are several useful resources for developing collaborative leaders and teams.

APPENDIX CONTENTS

COLLABORATIVE LEADERSHIP OPERATING PLATFORM

TEAM PRINCIPLES AND ESSENTIAL COMPETENCIES

Team Principles	Essential Competencies
Focus on Team, Not Position	Adaptability, Learning Agility
Understand That Everyone Can Play	Drive & Energy, Initiative, Functional/Technical Expertise
Embrace Diversity	Global Mind-Set, Relationship Building
Rely on Each Other	Relationship Building, Team Management, Team Player
Promote Both Individual & Team Values	Global Mind-Set, Integrity, Relationship Building
Seek Out Skillful, Adaptable Players	Adaptability, Learning Agility, Organizing & Planning
Charge the Team to Perform the Work	Customer Orientation, Results Orientation, Visioning
Empower Players to Win	Problem Solving & Decision Making, Risk Taking
Coach Teams to Respond to Changing Conditions on Their Own	Adaptability, Problem Solving & Decision Making[1], Communicativeness
Develop Partners on the Field	Communicativeness, Coaching, Delegation, Influence, Relationship Building
Achieve Cross-Cultural Agility	Global Mind-Set, Learning Agility, Relationship Building, Self-Objectivity

TEAM PRINCIPLE DESCRIPTIONS

Focus on Team, Not Position. Addresses the need to focus on results that can be produced when all team members effectively interact on the business field.

Understand That Everyone Can Play. Recognizes that technology is the great enabler that allows people everywhere to collaborate.

Embrace Diversity. Represents a prerequisite for partnering in global business, serves as a springboard for establishing trust, and brings strength to teams.

Rely on Each Other. Reinforces the team orientation, minimizes the silo mind-set, recognizes interdependency among team members, and supports genuine collaboration.

Promote Both Individual and Team Values. Deals with managing both values in a never-ending cycle to help ensure that the process employed to produce team results is working,

Seek Out Skillful, Adaptable Players. Promotes the need for flexibility when managing change, requires people and teams who can quickly assimilate and employ new skills and information, and recognizes that multiple skills are needed to perform effectively.

Charge the Team to Perform the Work. Recognizes the self-directed nature of the team charged with accomplishing the task or challenge and recognizes that the team is responsible for its own performance.

Empower Players to Win. Speaks to the commitment required to develop all team members and to provide continuous feedback with the goal of helping and encouraging them to make better decisions.

Coach Teams to Respond to Changing Conditions on Their Own. Reinforces the need to coach people on teams to manage their own performance in real-time under changing conditions for the purpose of producing positive results.

Develop Partners on the Field. Recognizes that all players on the business field are to be viewed as leaders and promotes the recognition of every opportunity as a leadership development step.

Achieve Cross-Cultural Agility. Calls for understanding the pivotal nature of relationships—and relationship building—to achieve positive results across cultures.

ESSENTIAL COMPETENCY DESCRIPTIONS[1]

Adaptability (Change Agility). Effective performers are adaptable. They embrace needed change and modify their behavior when appropriate to achieve organizational objectives. They are effective in the face of ambiguity. They understand and use change management techniques to help ensure smooth transitions.

Coaching. Effective performers partner with individuals in a thought-provoking and creative process that inspires them to maximize their personal and professional potential. They facilitate development by providing clear, behaviorally specific performance feedback and by making or eliciting specific suggestions for improvement in a manner that builds confidence and maintains self-esteem.

Communicativeness. Effective performers recognize the essential value of continuous information exchange and the competitive advantage it

---

1   See, Organization Systems International (www.orgsysint.com) to learn more about competencies included in the Polaris Competency Model

brings. They actively seek information from a variety of sources and disseminate it in a variety of ways. They use modern technologies to access and circulate information, even across great distances. They take responsibility for ensuring that their people have the current and accurate information needed for success.

Customer Orientation. Effective performers stay close to customers and consumers. They view the organization through the eyes of the customer and go out of their way to anticipate and meet customer needs. They continually seek out information and the opinions of respected others in order to better understand market trends.

Drive and Energy. Effective performers have a high level of energy and the motivation to sustain it over time. They are ambitious and passionate about their role in the organization. They have the stamina and endurance to handle the substantial workload present in today's organizations. They know that a healthy work/life balance is important to sustained energy. They are motivated to maintain a fast pace and they continue to produce, even in exhausting circumstances.

Delegation. Effective performers willingly entrust work to others. They provide clear guidelines and they monitor, redirect, and set limits as needed. They task others with challenging assignments whenever possible, sharing the authority and providing resources and support that empower others to meet their expectations.

Functional/Technical Expertise. Effective performers are knowledgeable and skilled in a functional specialty (e.g., finance, marketing, operations, information technologies, human resources, etc.). They add organizational value through unique expertise in a functional specialty area. They remain current in their area of expertise and serve as a resource in that area for the organization.

Global Mind-Set. Effective performers see their business in a global context. They look beyond their own borders for business opportunities and threats, and they have the transnational skills needed to manage across those borders. They welcome cross-cultural interactions and value differences among cultures.

Influence. Effective performers are skilled at directing, persuading, and motivating others. They are able to adapt their leadership style in order to direct, collaborate, or empower as the situation requires. They have established a personal power base built on mutual trust, fairness, and honesty.

Initiative. Effective performers are proactive and act without being prompted. They don't wait to be told what to do or when to do it. They see a need, take responsibility, and act on it. They make things happen.

Integrity. Effective performers think and act ethically and honestly. They apply ethical standards of behavior to daily work activities. They take responsibility for their actions and foster a work environment in which integrity is rewarded.

Learning Agility. Effective performers continuously seek new knowledge. They are curious and want to know "why." They learn quickly and use new information effectively. They create and foster a culture of interest, curiosity, and learning.

Organizing and Planning. Effective performers have strong organizing and planning skills that allow them to be highly productive and efficient. They manage their time wisely and they effectively prioritize multiple competing tasks. They plan, organize, and actively manage meetings for maximum productivity.

Problem Solving and Decision Making. Effective performers identify problems, solve them, act decisively, and show good judgment. They isolate causes from symptoms, and they compile information and alternatives to illuminate problems or issues. They involve others as appropriate, and they gather information from a variety of sources. They find a balance between studying the problem and solving it. They readily commit to action and make decisions that reflect sound judgment.

Relationship Building. Effective performers understand that a primary factor of success is the ability to establish and maintain productive relationships. They like interacting with people and are good at it. They devote appropriate time and energy to establishing and maintaining both individual contacts and networks, and they can utilize relationships to facilitate business transactions.

Results Orientation. Effective performers maintain appropriate focus on outcomes and accomplishments. They are motivated by achievement and they persist until their goal is reached. They convey a sense of urgency in order to make things happen. They respect the need to balance short-term and long-term goals. They are driven by a need for closure.

Risk Taking. Effective performers have a history of, and a propensity for, taking calculated chances to achieve goals. They find a balance between analysis and action. When they fail, they accept it, learn from it, and move on to the next challenge.

Self-Objectivity. Effective performers know their own strengths and limitations and are aware of their impact on others. They value self-knowledge and are open to feedback, using it for self-improvement.

Team Management. Effective performers create and maintain functional work units. They understand the human dynamics of team formation and maintenance. They formulate team roles and actively recruit and select team members in order to build effective work groups.

They develop and communicate clear team goals and roles, and they provide the level of guidance and management that is appropriate to each circumstance encountered. They reward team behavior and foster a team atmosphere in the workplace.

Team Player. Effective performers are team oriented. They identify with the larger organizational team and their role within it. They share resources, respond to requests from other parts of the organization, support larger legitimate organizational agendas, and view those larger agendas as more important than local or personal goals.

Visioning. Effective performers are imaginative. They can create a vision of a preferred future for their teams, and they communicate that vision clearly and enthusiastically in such a way that others are attracted to it. They can bring the vision to life for team members.

COLLABORATIVE LEADERSHIP COACHING

Team Mini-Charter

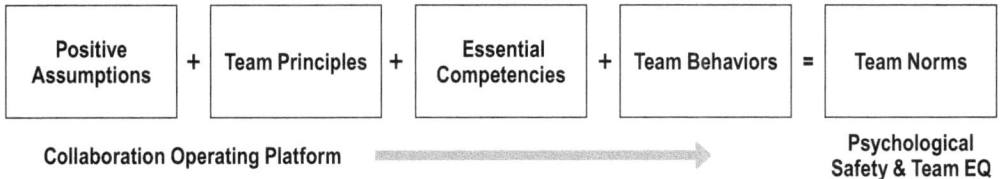

Positive Assumptions	+	Team Principles	+	Essential Competencies	+	Team Behaviors	=	Team Norms

Collaboration Operating Platform ⟶ Psychological Safety & Team EQ

COACH TO DEVELOP POSITIVE UNDERLYING ASSUMPTIONS

Your coaching here includes dealing with people who show up with underlying assumptions that support group work. If this is the case, your coaching starts with building your team's understanding that high performance is needed for the task at hand and that it can only be achieved when the team functions in a way that recognizes the interdependent nature of the team's relationship inside and outside of the team. Anything short of that would not result in high performance. (See "Your Underlying Assumptions," page 139.)

COACH TO DEVELOP A COLLABORATIVE MIND-SET

People on your team need to be coached on developing a collaborative mind-set to fully leverage the team's time and energy. This starts with the introduction of the team principles. The key is to convince the team to embed these principles in the team's charter in order to achieve high performance. This includes spending adequate time exploring, shaping, and agreeing on a charter that your team takes ownership in, both individually and collectively. This may be your key coaching challenge and one that requires ongoing communication. (See "Your Preference for Collaboration," page 140, and "What Does Collaboration Look Like for You?" page 141.)

If your team is described as an intact team working on multiple tasks, high performance may not be needed for each task the team is working on. In that case, members of the team may function in a way that does not recognize the interdependent nature of their relationship. This means that collaboration should *not* be your team's default for all tasks; instead, its application is task specific. As the team's leader, this is a management application you will have to address, when necessary. For project teams, high performance is the likely operational mode your team will take on to accomplish the task.

COACH TO DEVELOP A COLLABORATIVE SKILL SET

Once you've internalized the team principles, the next step involves developing the essential competencies focused on collaboration. By developing the competencies aligned with each team principle, you'll start to acquire a deeper understanding and appreciation of the mind-set needed to fully support the practice of genuine team collaboration.

The process for developing collaboration competencies is highly personalized. Here, your development should include learning what each competency is, as well as how it's used and developed.

Once you're comfortable with the language of competency development, the next move is to focus on diagnosis. Here, one option that's relatively easy to administer is to have you and/or people on your team rank which competencies are essential for each role. This is done by performing a card-sort exercise in which competencies from the inventory are sorted into three categories: exceptional, proficient, and needs development.

A second development option is to ask each person on your team to complete a self-assessment of all the competencies in the operating platform inventory. This will provide a simple, yet effective, way to pinpoint individual and team strengths and weaknesses. (See "Rate Your Proficiency: Collaborations Competencies," page 142.)

A third—and more involved—option is to schedule a 360° degree survey focused on essential competencies to capture feedback from people in your network (your supervisor, peers, and direct reports).

Last, you may elect to use the Big Six competencies to help jump-start your team's development.

Regardless of which option you use to identify knowledge or performance gaps, your ability to successfully apply the collaboration competencies is tied to being mindful of which competencies are aligned with each team principle.

COACH TO DEVELOP A COLLABORATIVE SKILL SET: THE BIG SIX

One short-term option for developing a collaborative skillset is the Big Six model. Developed by Bruce Griffiths, founder and president of Organization Systems International (OSI), this focused subset targets the competencies that are essential to exceptional performance in *frontline* managerial roles. The Big Six was created as a result of assessing thousands of high-performing leaders at more than 100 different organizations of all sizes and in many different markets over the course of forty years. To learn more about the Big Six, go to: www.orgsysint.com.

COACH TO DEVELOP TEAM EQ

Managers who don't succeed typically lack self-awareness, or EQ. The same can be said for teams. You should recognize that team EQ is a derivative of doing many things right. For example, you know how important fostering trust and building relationships are to team success.

You also know the importance of your team's charter, and you understand that positive underlying assumptions support the application of the team principles and essential competencies, eventually becoming habits for practicing genuine collaborative teamwork.

So, your coaching calls for a personal commitment to continue building your team's self-awareness as you collaborate to achieve results. Use the framework described in this section to help build and maintain psychological safety inside your team. This includes targeting selected competencies from the inventory provided in the team's operating platform.

Another coaching option is to use personality assessments such as the Myers-Briggs Type Indicator, or MBTI. The MBTI identifies people's preferences for taking in information, organizing work, communicating, and making decisions. I have used the MBTI for many years, both inside organizations where I worked and currently in my coaching and talent development work. It's been a great resource for building both individual and team self-awareness. For example, I've used the MBTI to describe and analyze a team, to help determine the root cause of a problem, to heighten team awareness, and to help sort through issues dealing with change management, communication, and even leadership. It's been especially useful in helping people on teams understand how to deal with conflict when it comes to decision-making styles. This is a critical area any team needs to master to be effective. Unfortunately for you as the team's coach, understanding and applying the MBTI takes training. Without it, your option is to bring in a team coach trained in MBTI who can help you facilitate this application with your team.

COACH TO DEVELOP COLLABORATIVE TEAM NORMS

The development of team norms is the third area where coaching will be highly beneficial. Because norms are established by teams and are used as ground rules for creating habits, your coaching should be centered on ensuring that your team's norms are serving to improve team effectiveness.

Meaningful team norms typically address how the team makes decisions, how goals are managed, and how the team promotes shared responsibility and accountability. Team decision making deals with building consensus and managing conflict. Goal setting addresses the need to manage shared agendas. And gaining commitments across the team deals with modeling the mind-set and behaviors you expect from others. These applications call for you to demonstrate inclusion in your actions as team coach. Without inclusiveness, there is no opportunity to tap into the talent on your team.

Because decision making is such a critical team norm, let's review a few key thoughts about it. First, the team's decision-making process will evoke a few emotions at times, prompting the need to manage conflict in a productive way. That's not always bad news, so long as the team's norm for managing conflict has been established and conflict is treated as healthy, thereby allowing people on the team to feel free to actively engage differences of opinion. Second, it's important to acknowledge that most new managers are not well equipped to manage conflict. I believe it is a specialized skill that calls for a commitment to developing conflict management skills as quickly as possible, so new managers need to jump in and get some conflict management training as soon as they can.

Psychological safety is another key team norm for developing and managing a culture of collaboration. This means, for example, that your coaching must be proactive and that people need to see your coaching presence to ensure high performance.

It's also important to recognize that the team's operating platform has three essential conditions embedded into its framework to support psychological safety leading to high performance, as described by Jacqueline Peters and Catherine Carr in their research: clear boundaries; a sense of meaning, urgency, and impact; and team competence. The first two conditions are addressed in the team principles and the third condition is covered by the essential competencies.

It's clear that *how* trumps *who* when it comes to team performance. In other words, the way in which people on the team work together is more important than who is on the team. When people are free to express themselves and take risks without feeling insecure or embarrassed, they have increased psychological safety.

COLLABORATIVE ASSESSMENTS

YOUR UNDERLYING ASSUMPTIONS

To determine whether the situation and management style is indicative of Theory X—Negative Assumptions or Theory Y—Positive Assumptions, score each of the statements below:

5 = Always   4 = Mostly   3 = Often   2 = Occasionally   1 = Rarely   0 = Never

1. My boss asks me politely to do things, gives me reasons why, and invites suggestions. ☐

2. I am encouraged to learn skills outside of my immediate area of responsibility. ☐

3. I am left to work without interference from my boss, but help is available if I want it. ☐

4. I am given credit and praise when I do good work or put in extra effort. ☐

5. People leaving the company are given an "exit interview" to hear their views on the organization. ☐

6. I am incentivized to work hard and well. ☐

7. If I want extra responsibility my boss will find a way to give it to me. ☐

8. If I want extra training, my boss will help me find how to get it or will arrange it. ☐

9. I call my boss and my boss's boss by their first names. ☐

10. My boss is available for me to discuss my concerns, worries, or suggestions. ☐

11. I know what the company's aims and targets are. ☐

12. I am told how the company plans to achieve its aims and targets. ☐

13. I am given an opportunity to solve problems connected with my work. ☐

14. My boss tells me what is happening within the organization. ☐

15. I have regular meetings with my boss to discuss how I can improve and develop. ☐

TOTAL ☐

60–75 = Strong Theory Y management (effective long term and short term)
45–59 = Predominately Theory Y management
16–44 = Predominately Theory X management
 0–15 = Strong Theory X management

YOUR PREFERENCE FOR COLLABORATION

To determine if you prefer being managed by a collaborative manager, score the statements below using the following scoring scale:

5 = Always   4 = Mostly   3 = Often   2 = Occasionally   1 = Rarely   0 = Never

1. I like to be involved and consulted by my boss about how I can best do my job. ☐
2. I want to learn skills outside of my immediate area of responsibility. ☐
3. I like to work without interference from my boss but be able to ask for help. ☐
4. I work best and most productively without pressure from my boss or threat of losing my job. ☐
5. When I leave the company, I would like an "exit interview" to give my views on the organization. ☐
6. I like to be incentivized and praised for working hard and well. ☐
7. I want to increase my responsibility. ☐
8. I want to be trained to do new things. ☐
9. I prefer to be friendly with my boss and the management. ☐
10. I want to be able to discuss my concerns, worries, or suggestions with my boss or another manager. ☐
11. I like to know what the company's aims and targets are. ☐
12. I like to be told how the company is performing on a regular basis. ☐
13. I like to be given opportunities to solve problems connected with my work. ☐
14. I like to be told by my boss what is happening in the organization. ☐
15. I like to have regular meetings with my boss to discuss how I can improve and develop. ☐

TOTAL ☐

60–75 = Strongly prefers collaboration
45–59 = Generally prefers collaboration
16–44 = Generally does not prefer collaboration
 0–15 = Strongly does not prefer collaboration

WHAT DOES COLLABORATION LOOK LIKE FOR YOU?

To determine whether your team principles match-up with a collaborative mind-set, check the team principles below that apply to you in your job (See "Team Principle Descriptions," pages 127–128):

OPERATING PRINCIPLE	YOU
1. Focus on Team, Not Position	☐
2. Understand That Everyone Can Play	☐
3. Embrace Diversity	☐
4. Rely on Each Other	☐
5. Promote Both Individual and Team Values	☐
6. Seek Out Skillful, Adaptable Players	☐
7. Charge the Team to Perform the Work	☐
8. Empower Players to Win	☐
9. Coach Teams to Respond to Changing Conditions on Their Own	☐
10. Develop Partners on the Field	☐
11. Achieve Cross-Cultural Agility	☐

TOTAL NUMBER PRINCIPLES CHECKED

RATE YOUR PROFICIENCY: ESSENTIAL COMPETENCIES

Rate yourself on the following competencies as they apply to your job or to a task you recently completed. Go with your *first* impression—don't spend time agonizing over your response.

Adaptability (Change Agility):

Needs Development   Proficient   Exceptional

{ }----------------------------{ }--------------------------------{ }

Coaching:

Needs Development   Proficient   Exceptional

{ }----------------------------{ }--------------------------------{ }

Communicativeness:

Needs Development   Proficient   Exceptional

{ }----------------------------{ }--------------------------------{ }

Customer Orientation:

Needs Development   Proficient   Exceptional

{ }----------------------------{ }--------------------------------{ }

Delegation:

Needs Development   Proficient   Exceptional

{ }----------------------------{ }--------------------------------{ }

Drive/Energy:

Needs Development   Proficient   Exceptional

{ }----------------------------{ }--------------------------------{ }

Functional/Technical Expertise:

Needs Development   Proficient   Exceptional

{ }----------------------------{ }--------------------------------{ }

Global Mind-Set:

Needs Development   Proficient   Exceptional

{ }----------------------------{ }--------------------------------{ }

Influence:

Needs Development   Proficient   Exceptional

{ }----------------------------{ }--------------------------------{ }

Initiative:

Needs Development   Proficient   Exceptional

{ }----------------------------{ }--------------------------------{ }

Integrity:

Needs Development   Proficient   Exceptional
{ }-----------------------------{ }-----------------------------------{ }

Learning Agility:

Needs Development   Proficient   Exceptional
{ }-----------------------------{ }-----------------------------------{ }

Organizing And Planning:

Needs Development   Proficient   Exceptional
{ }-----------------------------{ }-----------------------------------{ }

Problem Solving And Decision Making:

Needs Development   Proficient   Exceptional
{ }-----------------------------{ }-----------------------------------{ }

Relationship Building:

Needs Development   Proficient   Exceptional
{ }-----------------------------{ }-----------------------------------{ }

Results Orientation:

Needs Development   Proficient   Exceptional
{ }-----------------------------{ }-----------------------------------{ }

Risk Taking:

Needs Development   Proficient   Exceptional
{ }-----------------------------{ }-----------------------------------{ }

Self-Objecivity:

Needs Development   Proficient   Exceptional
{ }-----------------------------{ }-----------------------------------{ }

Team Management:

Needs Development   Proficient   Exceptional
{ }-----------------------------{ }-----------------------------------{ }

Team Player:

Needs Development   Proficient   Exceptional
{ }-----------------------------{ }-----------------------------------{ }

Visioning:

Needs Development   Proficient   Exceptional
{ }-----------------------------{ }-----------------------------------{ }